# Mastering SQL Server Administration: Performance, Security, and Maintenance

James Relington

## DEDICATION

To those who seek knowledge, inspiration, and new perspectives—
may this book be a companion on your journey, a spark for curiosity,
and a reminder that every page turned is a step toward discovery.

Introduction to SQL Server Administration ...........................................8

Setting Up SQL Server for Optimal Performance ..................................11

Configuring and Managing SQL Server Instances...............................15

SQL Server Database Architecture and Design............................19

Backup and Restore Strategies .................................................22

Understanding and Implementing Indexes ...........................................26

Performance Tuning and Query Optimization ..................................30

SQL Server Security Essentials ...............................................33

Implementing Authentication and Authorization ...........................37

SQL Server Encryption Techniques.......................................41

Managing and Auditing SQL Server Permissions................................45

Advanced SQL Server Security Features................................49

Optimizing SQL Server for High Availability ...................................52

Implementing and Managing SQL Server Clustering .........................56

Using SQL Server AlwaysOn Availability Groups ...............................60

Database Mirroring and Log Shipping ......................................64

SQL Server Replication and Synchronization.......................................67

Monitoring SQL Server Performance .....................................71

Identifying and Resolving Performance Bottlenecks .........................75

Advanced Query Optimization Techniques ...................................79

Managing SQL Server TempDB for Performance................................82

SQL Server Storage Optimization and Configuration ........................86

SQL Server Memory Management and Optimization ........................90

Understanding SQL Server Transaction Logs ....................................94

Automating SQL Server Administration Tasks ...................................97

SQL Server Agent and Job Management ...............................................101

Configuring and Using SQL Server Profiler ............................................ 105

Advanced Database Maintenance and Integrity Checks ..................... 109

Implementing SQL Server High Availability Solutions ....................... 112

Disaster Recovery Planning and Strategies ........................................... 116

SQL Server Performance Monitoring Tools ........................................... 120

Understanding SQL Server Query Plans ............................................... 123

SQL Server Data Compression Techniques .......................................... 127

SQL Server Cloud Integration and Hybrid Solutions ........................ 130

Implementing SQL Server in Virtualized Environments ................... 134

SQL Server Licensing and Cost Management ....................................... 138

Best Practices for SQL Server Deployment .......................................... 141

Troubleshooting SQL Server Errors and Issues .................................. 145

Automating SQL Server Backups and Restores ................................... 149

SQL Server Data Migration Strategies .................................................. 152

SQL Server Integration with PowerShell ............................................. 156

Upgrading and Patching SQL Server .................................................... 160

SQL Server Maintenance Plans and Best Practices ............................ 163

Data and Transaction Security in SQL Server .................................... 167

Auditing SQL Server for Compliance and Security ........................... 171

Implementing SQL Server Reporting and Analysis Tools ................. 174

Managing SQL Server on Linux ............................................................ 180

SQL Server Disaster Recovery with Azure Integration ..................... 183

SQL Server Troubleshooting Tools and Techniques .......................... 186

Designing Scalable SQL Server Architectures ..................................... 190

Future Trends in SQL Server Administration and Technologies ....... 193

# AKNOWLEDGEMENTS

I would like to express my deepest gratitude to everyone who contributed to the creation of this book. To my colleagues and mentors, your insights and expertise have been invaluable. A special thank you to my family and friends for their unwavering support and encouragement throughout this journey.

# Introduction to SQL Server Administration

SQL Server Administration is a critical aspect of managing data for businesses, organizations, and applications of all sizes. As a powerful relational database management system (RDBMS), SQL Server enables organizations to store, retrieve, manage, and analyze large amounts of structured data. For administrators, the primary focus lies in ensuring that the system runs smoothly, efficiently, and securely while maintaining high availability and performance. This chapter will introduce SQL Server administration, highlighting its key components and essential practices.

At the core of SQL Server administration is the database engine, which is responsible for processing and storing the data in a structured way. This engine is built to handle a vast range of tasks, from data retrieval to security and backup operations. Administrators work with several layers of the SQL Server environment, ranging from installation and configuration to ongoing monitoring and maintenance. They must ensure that the system is set up to support the business's requirements and can scale to accommodate future growth. Performance tuning is one of the first challenges administrators face, as they need to optimize the system to handle large volumes of transactions without degrading performance.

One of the primary responsibilities of an SQL Server administrator is the management of databases. A database is the container for all the data that an organization uses, and it must be designed, implemented, and maintained correctly. Proper database design is crucial for performance and maintainability. Administrators need to ensure that data is organized efficiently, indexed appropriately, and that data integrity is maintained through consistent use of keys and constraints. Furthermore, they must be proficient in using tools like SQL Server Management Studio (SSMS) to perform tasks such as creating, modifying, and deleting databases, as well as troubleshooting issues that may arise.

SQL Server also relies heavily on the concept of queries, which are commands written in Transact-SQL (T-SQL), SQL Server's proprietary extension of the SQL language. Queries are used to interact with the database, whether retrieving data, updating records, or performing complex calculations. The ability to optimize these queries is fundamental to achieving good performance, especially in large systems with complex workloads. Poorly optimized queries can result in slow performance, increased resource consumption, and even application downtime. As part of administration, SQL Server administrators must monitor query performance and use tools such as the SQL Server Profiler and Execution Plans to identify and address bottlenecks.

Security is another vital area of SQL Server administration. The integrity of the database and the data it stores must be protected at all costs. SQL Server offers a variety of security features that administrators can leverage, including authentication methods, user roles, and encryption. Properly implementing security measures ensures that sensitive data remains safe from unauthorized access or tampering. Administrators must regularly audit the system for security vulnerabilities, ensuring that permissions are granted according to the principle of least privilege, and that data is encrypted both at rest and in transit.

Backup and recovery are also critical aspects of SQL Server administration. Every database is susceptible to failure, whether due to hardware malfunction, human error, or malicious attack. Having a robust backup and recovery strategy in place is essential to prevent data loss and ensure business continuity. Administrators must set up regular backups of databases, transaction logs, and system configurations, and they must regularly test recovery processes to confirm that the system can be restored in the event of a disaster. SQL Server offers a variety of backup options, from full backups to differential and transaction log backups, each of which must be carefully configured to meet the needs of the organization.

Maintenance is a continuous process that must be monitored and updated to keep SQL Server running smoothly. Database maintenance tasks, such as rebuilding indexes, updating statistics, and checking for consistency, help to ensure that the database remains efficient and reliable. These tasks need to be automated whenever possible to minimize downtime and human error. Administrators must schedule these tasks regularly and check that they complete successfully. SQL Server includes tools such as Maintenance Plans and SQL Server Agent to automate many of these processes, reducing the administrative burden and freeing up resources for more strategic work.

Monitoring the health of the SQL Server system is an ongoing responsibility for administrators. This involves tracking the performance of the server, identifying potential issues before they impact users, and optimizing resources to maintain system stability. Administrators use monitoring tools to assess metrics such as CPU utilization, disk space usage, memory consumption, and query performance. The data from these tools helps to pinpoint areas where performance can be improved or where issues need to be addressed. Regular monitoring allows administrators to take proactive measures to maintain system health and avoid costly downtime.

SQL Server administration also involves a deep understanding of high availability and disaster recovery solutions. These solutions ensure that SQL Server remains operational even in the event of hardware failures or network outages. Technologies like AlwaysOn Availability Groups, database mirroring, and log shipping are commonly used to provide high availability and redundancy. By configuring and maintaining these solutions, administrators can minimize downtime and ensure that users have continuous access to critical data, even in the event of a failure.

The role of an SQL Server administrator is constantly evolving, as new features and technologies are introduced. SQL Server itself is a constantly evolving product, with each new version bringing enhancements to features like performance, security, and scalability. It is essential for administrators to stay up to date with the latest changes and best practices. This requires continuous learning and adaptation, as well as an understanding of the evolving needs of the business. Administrators must not only manage the current environment but also plan for future growth, scalability, and the integration of new technologies.

In conclusion, SQL Server administration is a multifaceted discipline that requires both technical expertise and strategic planning. From configuring and securing databases to monitoring performance and ensuring data availability, SQL Server administrators play a critical role in ensuring that the database environment runs smoothly. The ability to troubleshoot issues, optimize performance, and maintain system health is fundamental to the success of any organization that relies on SQL Server. As businesses continue to generate vast amounts of data, the need for skilled SQL Server administrators will only continue to grow, making it a rewarding and challenging career path.

# Setting Up SQL Server for Optimal Performance

Setting up SQL Server for optimal performance is a critical task for database administrators, as it ensures the system runs efficiently and supports the demanding workloads of modern applications. Proper configuration of SQL Server can have a profound impact on the database's responsiveness, reliability, and scalability. This chapter will discuss the key steps involved in configuring SQL Server for optimal performance, focusing on aspects such as hardware considerations, configuration settings, and database design.

The first step in setting up SQL Server for optimal performance begins with the hardware environment. SQL Server's performance is heavily dependent on the resources available to it, including CPU, memory, and storage. For the database engine to operate efficiently, the hardware must be tailored to meet the needs of the applications it supports. SQL Server requires significant computational power, especially when handling large datasets or high transaction volumes. Choosing the right CPU with multiple cores is essential for parallel processing, as SQL Server can execute queries across multiple cores to improve performance. Memory is equally important, as SQL Server uses it for caching data, query plans, and indexes. Insufficient memory can lead to excessive disk I/O and slower query execution times. The more memory available, the better SQL Server can perform, particularly with large databases and complex queries.

Storage performance is another key consideration when setting up SQL Server for optimal performance. The speed and configuration of the disks used for storing database files can greatly impact performance. SQL Server relies on fast disk I/O to retrieve and write data quickly. For this reason, it is important to configure multiple disk arrays to distribute the load of data storage, transaction logs, and backups. Placing the transaction log files on separate disks from the database files can improve performance by reducing contention for resources. Additionally, using Solid-State Drives (SSDs) for high-speed data access is highly recommended for environments with high transaction volumes or large datasets, as they provide significantly faster read and write speeds compared to traditional hard drives.

Once the hardware environment is properly set up, the next step is to configure SQL Server itself to optimize its performance. SQL Server offers a variety of configuration settings that can significantly impact the efficiency of database operations. One of the first settings that administrators should configure is the memory allocation for SQL Server. By default, SQL Server dynamically adjusts its memory usage, but in larger environments, it is often beneficial to manually configure the maximum amount of memory SQL Server can use to ensure that it does not consume too much system memory, potentially affecting other processes running on the server. Setting a maximum memory value helps prevent SQL Server from using all available memory, which can lead to system instability.

Another important configuration setting to consider is the parallelism option, which controls how SQL Server uses multiple processors to execute queries. The number of processors that SQL Server can use for parallel execution should be configured based on the server's CPU capabilities and the workload it is handling. For example, a server with many processors can benefit from increased parallelism, while a server with fewer processors may perform better with a more conservative configuration. Adjusting the maximum degree of parallelism (MAXDOP) setting can help SQL Server distribute queries efficiently across available processors, improving overall performance.

SQL Server also provides a feature called Auto Close, which is disabled by default but can be useful in certain scenarios. When enabled, Auto Close automatically shuts down the database after all connections are closed, releasing resources for other databases on the server. However, this feature can negatively impact performance if the database is frequently opened and closed, as it introduces overhead for each new connection. It is recommended to leave Auto Close disabled for production environments, as it can cause unnecessary delays.

Database design is an equally important aspect of setting up SQL Server for optimal performance. Even with the best hardware and configuration settings, poor database design can lead to suboptimal performance. Proper database schema design is essential for ensuring efficient data storage and retrieval. One of the most critical elements of database design is indexing. Indexes are used to speed up the retrieval of data by creating pointers to specific values within tables. Proper indexing can drastically improve query performance, especially for read-heavy applications. However, creating too many indexes can negatively impact performance, particularly when inserting, updating, or deleting records. Administrators must carefully consider which columns should be indexed, focusing on columns that are frequently queried or used in join operations.

Normalization is another key design principle that impacts performance. Normalization involves organizing data into multiple tables to reduce redundancy and ensure data integrity. While normalization is essential for ensuring a well-structured database, it is important to strike a balance between normalization and performance. Over-normalizing a database can result in excessive joins, which can degrade query performance. In some cases, denormalization, or reducing the level of normalization, may be necessary to improve query performance, particularly in reporting or data warehousing scenarios.

The use of stored procedures and views can also help optimize SQL Server performance. Stored procedures allow for precompiled queries to be executed, reducing the overhead of parsing and optimizing queries at runtime. Views, on the other hand, can simplify complex queries by encapsulating them in a virtual table. Both stored procedures and views can help streamline database operations and improve performance by reducing the amount of computation required at runtime.

In addition to design and configuration considerations, administrators should also focus on monitoring and tuning SQL Server's performance regularly. SQL Server provides a range of tools and reports for monitoring performance, such as the SQL Server Management Studio (SSMS) Performance Dashboard, SQL Server Profiler, and Dynamic Management Views (DMVs). These tools allow administrators to identify bottlenecks, such as slow-running queries, excessive CPU usage, or high disk I/O, and take appropriate action to resolve them. Query optimization is an ongoing task, and administrators must be vigilant in analyzing execution plans, tuning queries, and adjusting indexing strategies as needed to maintain optimal performance.

Regular maintenance tasks, such as updating statistics, rebuilding indexes, and checking for database consistency, are also crucial to maintaining optimal performance. SQL Server provides several maintenance features, such as the Maintenance Plan Wizard and SQL Server Agent, which automate these tasks and reduce the administrative burden. By automating maintenance tasks, administrators can ensure that the database remains in good health and continues to perform efficiently.

Setting up SQL Server for optimal performance is an ongoing process that involves careful planning, configuration, and ongoing monitoring. By focusing on hardware considerations, fine-tuning SQL Server configuration settings, implementing sound database design practices, and maintaining the system regularly, administrators can ensure that SQL Server delivers the best possible performance for their organization's needs. Optimizing SQL Server is not a one-time task but rather a continuous effort to adapt to changing workloads and evolving technology. Through regular monitoring, proactive tuning, and thoughtful design, administrators can ensure that SQL Server remains a high-performing, reliable database solution.

# Configuring and Managing SQL Server Instances

Configuring and managing SQL Server instances is a fundamental aspect of SQL Server administration that directly impacts the performance, security, and reliability of the database environment. A SQL Server instance refers to a complete installation of SQL Server that operates independently and can host multiple databases. Instances provide a way to isolate different workloads and configurations, enabling administrators to fine-tune the system for specific purposes. This chapter will explore the key aspects of configuring and managing SQL Server instances, focusing on installation, configuration settings, management tasks, and monitoring.

The process of setting up a SQL Server instance begins with installation. During the installation, administrators are prompted to choose a variety of options that will affect the behavior of the SQL Server instance. One of the most important decisions during installation is selecting the instance type. SQL Server offers two primary types of instances: default and named. A default instance is installed with a predefined name, typically "MSSQLSERVER," and can only be accessed using the server's hostname or IP address. Named instances, on the other hand, allow administrators to install multiple SQL Server instances on a single server, each with a unique name. Named instances provide greater flexibility, particularly in environments where multiple applications or departments require isolated database environments. Properly choosing between a default or named instance is critical for the effective management of SQL Server in larger environments.

Once the SQL Server instance is installed, administrators must configure the instance to meet the specific needs of the organization.

One of the first configuration tasks is setting up the server properties, which control various aspects of how SQL Server operates. These properties include memory allocation, CPU usage, and file locations, among others. Adjusting the memory settings ensures that SQL Server has access to enough system resources to perform efficiently while also preventing it from consuming excessive memory and impacting other applications on the server. For large databases or high-transaction environments, configuring the instance to maximize memory usage can help improve performance by reducing the need for disk I/O.

Another critical configuration task is setting up the server's authentication mode. SQL Server supports two types of authentication: Windows authentication and mixed-mode authentication. Windows authentication is the preferred method for most environments, as it leverages Active Directory to authenticate users and grants access based on Windows user accounts. Mixed-mode authentication, which allows both Windows and SQL Server authentication, is often used in environments where SQL Server-based logins are required. Administrators should carefully consider the security implications of their authentication choice and ensure that only necessary users and groups are granted access to the SQL Server instance.

Once authentication is configured, administrators must focus on security settings. SQL Server provides a range of security options to protect the database and its contents from unauthorized access. Server-level security begins with configuring SQL Server logins, which are used to grant users access to the server and its databases. Administrators must assign appropriate permissions to logins based on the principle of least privilege, ensuring that users only have the necessary permissions to perform their tasks. It is also important to configure roles and schemas within SQL Server to manage access to specific objects, such as tables and views, more effectively. Regular auditing and monitoring of login activity and permissions can help ensure that security remains tight and that any unauthorized attempts to access the instance are detected.

Database management tasks play a key role in maintaining the health of a SQL Server instance. Once an instance is up and running, administrators must monitor its performance and address any issues that arise. SQL Server provides a range of tools to assist with performance monitoring, including SQL Server Management Studio (SSMS), SQL Server Profiler, and Dynamic Management Views (DMVs). These tools enable administrators to track performance metrics such as CPU usage, memory consumption, and query execution times. By regularly reviewing these metrics, administrators can identify performance bottlenecks and take corrective action. For example, if a particular query is causing high CPU utilization, administrators may need to optimize the query or create an index to improve its performance.

One of the most common tasks associated with managing SQL Server instances is ensuring that databases are properly backed up. Regular backups are essential to protect against data loss due to hardware failure, corruption, or user error. SQL Server provides a variety of backup options, including full, differential, and transaction log backups. Administrators should configure automated backup schedules to ensure that backups are performed regularly and that they are stored in a secure location. It is also crucial to test the restore process periodically to ensure that backups can be successfully restored in the event of a disaster.

Managing SQL Server instances also involves handling routine maintenance tasks, such as rebuilding indexes, updating statistics, and checking for database consistency. Over time, indexes can become fragmented, which can lead to slower query performance. Rebuilding or reorganizing indexes regularly can help maintain optimal performance. Similarly, updating statistics ensures that SQL Server's query optimizer has up-to-date information about the data distribution in the database, allowing it to generate more efficient query plans. Regular database consistency checks using tools like DBCC CHECKDB help identify and repair corruption that may occur over time.

Another important management task is managing the SQL Server Agent, which automates administrative tasks such as backup jobs, index maintenance, and data import/export. The SQL Server Agent is a powerful tool that allows administrators to create jobs that can run at scheduled times or in response to specific events. Administrators can use the SQL Server Agent to automate many of the repetitive tasks associated with instance management, reducing the likelihood of human error and ensuring that maintenance tasks are performed consistently.

Monitoring SQL Server instances is an ongoing responsibility. In addition to performance metrics, administrators must also monitor the health of the instance itself, including the status of system processes, disk space availability, and error logs. SQL Server provides tools like SQL Server Management Studio (SSMS) and SQL Server Profiler to capture and analyze events that may indicate problems with the instance. Error logs are an invaluable resource for diagnosing issues, as they record critical information about the instance's operations, including startup and shutdown events, backup activities, and error messages. By regularly reviewing error logs, administrators can proactively address issues before they escalate into more significant problems.

When managing multiple instances of SQL Server, administrators must also consider the complexity of managing and maintaining each instance. SQL Server provides tools such as SQL Server Management Studio (SSMS) and PowerShell scripts to help administrators manage multiple instances from a single interface. Using centralized management tools, administrators can monitor the health of all instances, perform routine maintenance, and implement configuration changes across multiple servers simultaneously.

In addition to managing local instances, administrators may also need to configure and manage instances that are part of a distributed environment. SQL Server can be configured for high availability and disaster recovery using technologies such as AlwaysOn Availability Groups, database mirroring, or log shipping. These configurations help ensure that SQL Server instances are resilient and can continue operating even in the event of a failure.

Configuring and managing SQL Server instances is a comprehensive task that requires careful planning, monitoring, and maintenance. By properly configuring instances during installation, optimizing settings for performance, managing security, and automating administrative tasks, administrators can ensure that SQL Server instances remain efficient, secure, and reliable. Through ongoing monitoring and maintenance, administrators can address performance issues, ensure data integrity, and keep the SQL Server environment running smoothly.

# SQL Server Database Architecture and Design

SQL Server database architecture and design are fundamental aspects of building a robust, scalable, and efficient database system. The design decisions made during the creation of a database can significantly affect its performance, maintainability, and scalability. Understanding SQL Server's architecture is critical for administrators, developers, and architects to ensure that the database system is optimized for the needs of the business. This chapter will delve into the key elements of SQL Server's database architecture and the principles of designing an effective database.

At the core of SQL Server's database architecture is the relational model, which organizes data into tables that consist of rows and columns. Each table represents a specific entity or object, and the columns represent the attributes of that entity. This structure allows SQL Server to store, retrieve, and manipulate data in a way that is both flexible and efficient. The relational model also ensures that data is stored in a structured format that makes it easy to manage and query.

SQL Server uses a system of databases to organize and store data. A database in SQL Server consists of multiple objects, including tables, indexes, views, stored procedures, and triggers. Each database is housed within a specific instance of SQL Server and is managed by the database engine. SQL Server's database engine handles the storage, retrieval, and management of data, ensuring that operations such as insertions, deletions, updates, and queries are performed efficiently. The database engine also enforces integrity constraints to ensure that data remains consistent and accurate.

A key aspect of SQL Server's architecture is the transaction log, which tracks all changes made to the database. Every time data is modified, an entry is made in the transaction log. This log ensures that changes are durable and can be rolled back in the event of a failure, providing a mechanism for database recovery. The transaction log plays a critical role in maintaining the consistency of the database, ensuring that changes are either fully committed or rolled back without leaving the database in an inconsistent state.

SQL Server databases are stored in a set of files, primarily consisting of data files and log files. Data files store the actual data and can be further divided into primary data files (with the extension .mdf) and secondary data files (with the extension .ndf). The primary data file contains the system information, while secondary data files store additional data for larger databases. Log files, on the other hand, are used to store the transaction log, which records all changes made to the database. The log files have the extension .ldf and are critical for the recovery process in case of system failure.

The SQL Server database engine relies on a combination of physical and logical storage structures to optimize data retrieval and performance. One of the primary physical structures is the page, which is the smallest unit of data storage in SQL Server. A page is typically 8 KB in size and is used to store rows of data. Pages are organized into extents, which are groups of eight pages. These extents help SQL Server manage data storage and allocation more efficiently.

To enhance performance, SQL Server employs indexing, which provides a faster way to retrieve data. Indexes are created on one or more columns of a table and act as pointers to the data, allowing SQL Server to quickly locate specific rows. The most common type of index is the clustered index, which determines the physical order of rows in a table. Non-clustered indexes are separate from the data and provide an alternate way of accessing the data. Indexing is an essential component of SQL Server's architecture, as it can significantly improve query performance, especially for read-heavy applications.

When designing a SQL Server database, one of the first considerations is normalization, which involves organizing data to reduce redundancy and improve data integrity. Normalization divides data into multiple related tables, minimizing the need for repetitive data. This process helps maintain consistency, as any update to a piece of data only needs to be made in one place. However, normalization can sometimes lead to performance issues, especially when data retrieval involves many joins. Therefore, database designers must strike a balance between normalization and performance. In some cases, denormalization, or the process of combining tables to reduce the number of joins, may be necessary to improve query performance.

Another important aspect of database design is the use of foreign keys to maintain referential integrity. A foreign key is a column or set of columns that establishes a relationship between two tables. This relationship ensures that the data in the related tables remains consistent. For example, a foreign key constraint can prevent a record from being inserted into a child table if there is no corresponding record in the parent table. This helps maintain data integrity by ensuring that relationships between entities are always valid.

In addition to foreign keys, SQL Server allows designers to use triggers and stored procedures to enforce business logic and automate tasks. Triggers are special types of stored procedures that automatically execute in response to certain events, such as insertions, updates, or deletions. Triggers can be used to enforce rules, such as updating related data in another table or preventing invalid data from being inserted. Stored procedures, on the other hand, allow for precompiled SQL code that can be executed repeatedly. They are commonly used to encapsulate complex queries or business logic, helping to improve maintainability and reusability.

Concurrency control is another important aspect of database design. In a multi-user environment, multiple transactions may attempt to access the same data simultaneously. SQL Server provides mechanisms for managing concurrency and ensuring that transactions are executed in a way that preserves the integrity of the database. One of these mechanisms is locking, which prevents other transactions from modifying data that is being used by another transaction. SQL Server uses various types of locks, including shared, exclusive, and update locks, to control access to data. While locking is essential for data consistency, it can also lead to performance issues such as blocking, where transactions are delayed because they are waiting for locks to be released.

A well-designed SQL Server database must also take into account the scalability and availability needs of the organization. As data volumes grow, the database must be able to scale to handle increasing loads. SQL Server provides several features to support scalability, such as partitioning, which divides large tables into smaller, more manageable pieces, and replication, which allows data to be copied across multiple servers for high availability. Additionally, AlwaysOn Availability Groups provide a high-availability solution by replicating databases across multiple instances of SQL Server, ensuring that data remains available even in the event of a server failure.

Security is another critical aspect of SQL Server database design. The design must account for who has access to the data and how that access is controlled. SQL Server provides multiple layers of security, including authentication, authorization, and encryption. Administrators must design the database with the principle of least privilege in mind, granting users only the permissions necessary for their tasks. Furthermore, data encryption can be used to protect sensitive information both at rest and in transit.

Designing a SQL Server database is not just about technical considerations; it also involves understanding the business requirements and ensuring that the database supports the goals of the organization. A well-designed database will be able to scale as needed, perform efficiently, and remain secure, while also providing a solid foundation for the applications that depend on it. Whether the database is supporting transactional processing, analytics, or reporting, the architecture and design choices made early on will play a crucial role in the success of the SQL Server deployment.

# Backup and Restore Strategies

Backup and restore strategies are fundamental components of SQL Server database administration, ensuring that data can be protected and recovered in the event of a failure, corruption, or other disasters. An effective backup strategy involves understanding the different types of backups available, when to use them, and how to plan for a recovery that minimizes downtime and data loss. Similarly, an efficient restore strategy ensures that data can be recovered quickly and accurately. This chapter will explore the essential aspects of backup and restore strategies in SQL Server, including the types of backups, best practices, and considerations for optimizing the backup and recovery process.

The primary goal of any backup strategy is to protect the data from loss. SQL Server provides several types of backups, each serving a different purpose and offering varying levels of granularity and recovery speed. The most basic type of backup is the full backup, which contains all the data in the database at the time the backup is taken. A full backup captures the entire database, including all data files, system objects, and other components necessary for a complete recovery. Full backups are essential as the foundation of any backup strategy, providing a point-in-time snapshot of the database. However, while full backups provide comprehensive protection, they can be time-consuming and resource-intensive to perform, especially for large databases.

In addition to full backups, SQL Server supports differential backups, which back up only the data that has changed since the last full backup. Differential backups provide a more efficient method of backing up data by capturing only the incremental changes, reducing the time and storage required compared to full backups. They are typically used in conjunction with full backups to offer a balance between backup time and recovery time. By regularly taking differential backups, administrators can reduce the time it takes to restore a database to the most recent point in time, as only the last full backup and the most recent differential backup are needed for recovery.

Another type of backup in SQL Server is the transaction log backup, which records all changes made to the database since the last transaction log backup. Transaction log backups are critical for maintaining the consistency and integrity of the database, as they allow for point-in-time recovery. Transaction logs enable database administrators to restore a database to a specific point in time, even down to the minute or second, by replaying the changes recorded in the transaction logs. In environments where high availability and minimal data loss are critical, transaction log backups are an essential component of the backup strategy. They are typically taken on a frequent basis, such as every few minutes or hours, to ensure that changes are consistently captured.

The combination of full, differential, and transaction log backups forms the backbone of a robust SQL Server backup strategy. By using these different backup types together, administrators can minimize downtime and data loss while ensuring that recovery is possible in a variety of scenarios. It is important to consider the frequency of each backup type to balance performance, storage, and recovery time. For instance, a full backup might be scheduled weekly, differential backups daily, and transaction log backups every few hours or more frequently, depending on the level of activity and the business's recovery requirements.

Backup storage is another critical aspect of an effective backup strategy. SQL Server provides several options for storing backups, including local storage, network-attached storage (NAS), and cloud-based solutions. Each option has its advantages and trade-offs in terms of cost, performance, and reliability. Local storage offers fast access to backups but may not provide the redundancy needed for disaster recovery. Network storage offers more flexibility and scalability, while cloud-based solutions provide off-site storage that can be accessed in the event of a physical disaster. A multi-tiered approach that combines on-site and off-site backup storage is often the most effective strategy for ensuring that backups are both secure and easily accessible.

Backup compression is a feature in SQL Server that can help reduce the size of backup files, making backups faster and more efficient. Compressed backups consume less disk space and can be transferred more quickly, which is particularly important when dealing with large databases or limited network bandwidth. However, compression comes with a performance overhead, as SQL Server must spend additional resources to compress the data. Administrators should assess the trade-offs between backup speed, storage requirements, and performance when deciding whether to use compression in their backup strategy.

In addition to regular backups, administrators must also ensure that backup integrity is maintained over time. Backup verification is essential to ensure that backups can be restored successfully when needed. SQL Server offers tools such as the CHECKSUM and VERIFYONLY options, which can be used to validate the integrity of backup files. Regularly testing restores from backups is another critical practice, as it helps identify potential issues before a disaster strikes. By periodically performing test restores, administrators can ensure that the restore process works as expected and that backups are reliable.

When it comes to restoring SQL Server databases, the goal is to minimize downtime and data loss while ensuring that recovery is as efficient as possible. SQL Server provides various restore options, depending on the type of backup and the desired recovery point. A simple restore operation involves restoring the most recent full backup, followed by any differential backups and transaction log backups that are needed to bring the database up to the desired point in time. SQL Server also supports point-in-time recovery, which allows administrators to restore a database to a specific moment, such as just before a failure or data corruption occurred. Point-in-time recovery is made possible by transaction log backups, which record all changes to the database and allow the administrator to roll the database forward to the precise moment of recovery.

In high-availability environments, SQL Server provides features such as database mirroring, AlwaysOn Availability Groups, and log shipping to enhance the recovery process. These features allow for automatic or manual failover, reducing downtime and providing continuous access to data in the event of a failure. Database mirroring, for example, maintains a copy of the database on a secondary server, and if the primary server fails, the secondary server can take over without requiring a full restore. AlwaysOn Availability Groups offer even more advanced high-availability and disaster recovery capabilities by replicating databases across multiple servers, providing both automatic failover and disaster recovery without requiring manual intervention.

An often-overlooked aspect of backup and restore strategies is managing the backup retention policy. Over time, backup files can accumulate, consuming valuable storage space. Administrators must establish a retention policy that specifies how long to keep each backup type and when to delete or archive old backups. The retention policy should be aligned with business requirements, legal compliance, and recovery objectives. Archiving older backups to more cost-effective storage solutions, such as tape or cloud storage, can help reduce storage costs while ensuring that historical backups are still accessible if needed.

Backup and restore strategies are critical for ensuring the availability and protection of data in SQL Server environments. A well-designed backup strategy leverages a combination of full, differential, and transaction log backups to provide comprehensive data protection while balancing performance, storage, and recovery time. By utilizing the right backup storage solutions, verifying backup integrity, and regularly testing restores, administrators can ensure that data is recoverable in any situation. Furthermore, understanding SQL Server's restore capabilities and high-availability features can help minimize downtime and data loss, ensuring business continuity and maintaining the integrity of the database system.

# Understanding and Implementing Indexes

Indexes are a critical component of SQL Server's architecture, playing a significant role in improving the performance of data retrieval operations. They function as a roadmap to quickly locate data within a database, making queries more efficient and reducing the time required to search through large tables. However, while indexes offer significant performance benefits, their implementation and management must be carefully considered to avoid potential downsides such as increased storage requirements and slower write operations. This chapter will delve into the fundamentals of SQL Server indexing, exploring how indexes work, the types of indexes available, and best practices for implementing and maintaining them.

At its core, an index in SQL Server is a data structure that provides a fast lookup of rows in a database table. Without an index, SQL Server must perform a full table scan to find the data that matches a query's criteria. A full table scan involves reading each row in the table, which can be time-consuming, especially for large tables. An index eliminates the need for a full scan by creating a sorted list of the values in one or more columns, allowing SQL Server to quickly locate the desired rows. The index structure typically organizes the data in a tree-like structure known as a B-tree, where each leaf node of the tree contains a pointer to the actual row in the table.

The most common type of index is the clustered index, which determines the physical order of rows in the table. When a clustered index is created on a table, the data rows are rearranged to match the order of the indexed column(s). Each table can have only one clustered index because the data rows can only be physically sorted in one way. The clustered index is typically created on the primary key column, but it can also be created on other columns that are frequently used in queries to filter or sort data. One of the key advantages of clustered indexes is that they significantly improve the performance of queries that retrieve data in a sorted order, as the data is already organized in the desired order.

Non-clustered indexes are another type of index in SQL Server. Unlike clustered indexes, non-clustered indexes do not affect the physical order of rows in the table. Instead, a non-clustered index creates a separate structure that stores the indexed columns and a pointer to the corresponding data row in the table. A table can have multiple non-clustered indexes, each providing a different way to access the data. Non-clustered indexes are typically used to speed up queries that involve filtering, joining, or sorting on columns that are not the primary key. While non-clustered indexes provide significant performance improvements, they also come with the overhead of additional storage space and maintenance, as the index must be updated whenever the underlying data is modified.

SQL Server also supports unique indexes, which enforce the uniqueness of the values in the indexed columns. A unique index ensures that no two rows in the table can have the same value in the indexed columns, providing a mechanism for data integrity. Unique indexes are often created automatically when a primary key or unique constraint is defined on a table. While unique indexes are similar to non-clustered indexes, they differ in that they enforce uniqueness and prevent the insertion of duplicate values in the indexed columns.

Filtered indexes are a special type of non-clustered index that allows administrators to create an index on a subset of data in a table, based on a filter condition. Filtered indexes are useful when only a small portion of the data in a table is frequently queried, as they reduce the size of the index and improve query performance by focusing on the relevant data. For example, a filtered index could be created on a table that stores customer orders to include only orders that are marked as "shipped," improving the performance of queries that filter for shipped orders.

Full-text indexes provide a way to index large text-based data, such as descriptions, documents, or articles, and enable advanced searching capabilities. Full-text indexes are designed to handle unstructured data, such as text fields, and provide features like word-based searches, stemming, and proximity searches. Full-text indexes are typically used in scenarios where users need to search large amounts of text quickly, such as in content management systems, product catalogs, or customer support systems.

When implementing indexes in SQL Server, administrators must carefully consider which columns to index. Indexing is most beneficial for columns that are frequently used in WHERE clauses, JOIN conditions, or ORDER BY clauses. These columns are typically candidates for creating clustered or non-clustered indexes. However, creating too many indexes can lead to performance issues, as each index must be updated whenever data is inserted, updated, or deleted. Index maintenance can become a resource-intensive task, especially in tables with frequent write operations. As a result, it is essential to strike a balance between improving query performance and minimizing the impact on write operations.

Another important consideration when implementing indexes is the order of columns within a multi-column index. The order of columns in an index can have a significant impact on query performance, as SQL Server will use the index in the most efficient way possible based on the order of columns. When creating a multi-column index, administrators should place the most selective columns first. A column is considered selective if it contains a large number of distinct values, as these columns help SQL Server filter the data more effectively. Placing selective columns first allows SQL Server to reduce the number of rows it needs to process when executing a query, resulting in faster query execution times.

Regular maintenance of indexes is crucial to ensure optimal performance over time. As data is inserted, updated, and deleted, indexes can become fragmented. Fragmentation occurs when the logical order of the index no longer matches its physical order, leading to inefficient use of storage and slower query performance. SQL Server provides tools for identifying index fragmentation and for reorganizing or rebuilding indexes to improve performance. Reorganizing an index is a less resource-intensive operation that defragments the index without rebuilding it, while rebuilding an index creates a new index structure from scratch. In highly transactional environments, it may be necessary to rebuild indexes regularly to ensure optimal performance.

SQL Server also provides the option to manage index maintenance automatically through maintenance plans, which can be scheduled to run at regular intervals. These plans can include tasks such as index rebuilding, updating statistics, and checking database consistency. By automating index maintenance, administrators can ensure that indexes are kept in optimal condition without manual intervention.

Another important aspect of indexing is monitoring the performance of indexes. SQL Server provides several Dynamic Management Views (DMVs) that allow administrators to track the usage of indexes and identify which indexes are being used and which are not. Indexes that are not used frequently may be candidates for removal, as they add unnecessary overhead in terms of storage and maintenance. On the other hand, indexes that are frequently used but are fragmented may need to be rebuilt or reorganized to maintain performance.

In environments with large databases or complex queries, index design becomes a critical factor in performance optimization. Properly implemented indexes can significantly reduce query response times, improve throughput, and reduce server load. However, index design should be approached with careful consideration of the specific workload and query patterns, as well as the impact on write operations. By understanding the different types of indexes and their appropriate use cases, administrators can create a balanced index strategy that optimizes query performance while minimizing the cost of index maintenance. Effective index management can have a profound impact on the overall efficiency and scalability of SQL Server, ensuring that databases remain performant and responsive as data volumes and query complexity grow.

# Performance Tuning and Query Optimization

Performance tuning and query optimization are essential practices for SQL Server administrators and developers to ensure that database systems operate efficiently, even as data grows and query complexity increases. Poorly performing queries and inefficient database configurations can lead to significant delays, system slowdowns, and a negative impact on the overall user experience. This chapter delves into the techniques and strategies involved in performance tuning and query optimization, helping database professionals improve the efficiency and responsiveness of SQL Server environments.

The first step in performance tuning is understanding how SQL Server processes queries. When a query is executed, the SQL Server query optimizer is responsible for determining the most efficient way to execute it. The query optimizer evaluates multiple potential execution plans and selects the one that it believes will yield the fastest results. The optimizer relies on statistics and indexes to make these decisions, and if the statistics are outdated or missing, or if the indexes are not well-designed, the optimizer might choose a suboptimal execution plan. This is why regularly updating statistics and ensuring that the right indexes are in place are fundamental practices for maintaining optimal performance.

One of the most common sources of query performance issues is the inefficient use of indexes. Indexes are crucial for speeding up data retrieval, but if they are poorly designed or not used effectively, they can actually hinder performance. For example, a query that accesses a table without an appropriate index will require a full table scan, which is much slower than using an index. Additionally, having too many indexes on a table can also cause performance issues, particularly during data modifications such as inserts, updates, and deletes, as SQL Server must maintain each index every time the underlying data changes. Striking a balance between having enough indexes to improve query performance and not overloading the system with unnecessary indexes is a critical aspect of query optimization.

Once indexes are properly configured, it is important to focus on the structure of the queries themselves. Query optimization involves writing efficient queries that minimize resource consumption while still returning the correct results. One of the key practices in query optimization is eliminating unnecessary complexity. For example, using subqueries or joins that are not needed can increase the execution time of a query. A query that includes a subquery, for instance, can often be rewritten as a join, which is typically more efficient. Similarly, using the SELECT * statement can be wasteful, as it retrieves all columns from a table, even if only a few are needed. By explicitly specifying the required columns, the query can run more efficiently and reduce the amount of data transferred.

Another important query optimization technique is reducing the number of rows that need to be processed. This can be achieved by adding appropriate WHERE clauses that filter out unnecessary rows early in the query execution. For example, applying filters in the WHERE clause can significantly reduce the number of rows that SQL Server needs to scan and process, which can lead to faster query execution. Additionally, using appropriate joins and avoiding Cartesian joins, which can result in large, unfiltered result sets, is essential for maintaining efficient queries.

SQL Server also provides a range of tools to help identify and address performance bottlenecks. One of the most powerful tools is the Execution Plan, which shows the steps SQL Server takes to execute a query. By analyzing the execution plan, administrators can identify areas where the query is inefficient, such as expensive table scans, missing indexes, or suboptimal join strategies. The execution plan provides insights into how SQL Server processes each part of the query, allowing administrators to pinpoint specific issues that need to be addressed. Using the SQL Server Management Studio (SSMS), administrators can view the execution plan for a query and look for costly operations like sort, hash match, or nested loop joins, which can be optimized to improve performance.

In addition to execution plans, SQL Server also provides Dynamic Management Views (DMVs), which offer real-time insights into query performance. DMVs provide information about query execution statistics, including the number of reads and writes, the execution time, and the frequency of execution. By querying the DMVs, administrators can identify long-running queries, queries that consume excessive resources, and queries that may benefit from optimization. These views are invaluable for proactively monitoring and optimizing query performance in production environments.

Another important area of performance tuning is optimizing the database schema. A well-designed schema can reduce query complexity and improve performance by ensuring that data is stored in a way that minimizes the need for complex joins or excessive data retrieval. Normalization is a common practice in database design that helps eliminate redundancy and ensures data integrity. However, excessive normalization can sometimes lead to performance issues, particularly when queries require multiple joins. In such cases, denormalization, or combining tables to reduce the number of joins, may be necessary to improve performance.

The size and structure of the database can also impact performance. Large tables with millions of rows can lead to slow query performance, particularly if queries involve searching through large amounts of data. One way to improve performance in such cases is by partitioning large tables. Partitioning involves splitting a large table into smaller, more manageable pieces, known as partitions, which can be queried independently. This reduces the amount of data that needs to be scanned for each query and can lead to faster query execution. Partitioning is especially useful in scenarios where data is often queried by date ranges, such as in time-series data, as it allows SQL Server to access only the relevant partitions instead of scanning the entire table.

Caching is another optimization technique that can significantly improve query performance. SQL Server uses an in-memory buffer pool to cache data and execution plans. By keeping frequently accessed data and query plans in memory, SQL Server can avoid having to read from disk, which is much slower. However, if the buffer pool is too small, SQL Server may have to read from disk more frequently, leading to slower query performance. Administrators can monitor buffer pool usage and adjust the configuration to ensure that SQL Server has enough memory to cache frequently accessed data. In addition, query plans are cached to avoid recompiling queries every time they are executed. However, poorly cached plans can also degrade performance, so it is important to monitor and manage the cache to ensure optimal plan reuse.

Concurrency is another critical factor in query optimization. In a multi-user environment, multiple transactions may attempt to access the same data simultaneously, which can lead to contention and performance degradation. SQL Server provides several mechanisms to manage concurrency, such as locking and isolation levels. Locks prevent other transactions from modifying data that is being accessed by another transaction, ensuring data consistency. However, excessive locking can lead to blocking, where one query is delayed because it is waiting for another query to release its lock. To minimize blocking and improve concurrency, administrators can adjust isolation levels, use appropriate indexes, and optimize queries to reduce the need for locking.

Performance tuning and query optimization are continuous processes that require regular monitoring, analysis, and adjustment. By leveraging SQL Server's powerful tools like execution plans, DMVs, and indexing strategies, administrators can identify and address performance bottlenecks. Additionally, by writing efficient queries, optimizing the database schema, and managing concurrency effectively, administrators can ensure that SQL Server operates at peak performance. The goal is to create a balanced environment where data retrieval is fast, efficient, and scalable, even as data volumes and query complexity grow.

# SQL Server Security Essentials

SQL Server security is a fundamental concern for database administrators, developers, and organizations as a whole. The integrity and confidentiality of data must be ensured in order to protect sensitive information from unauthorized access, modification, and disclosure. SQL Server provides a wide range of security features designed to help secure the database environment, protect data both at rest and in transit, and ensure that access to the database is controlled in a way that aligns with best practices and organizational policies. This chapter will explore the core components of SQL Server security, including authentication, authorization, encryption, and auditing.

The first line of defense in SQL Server security is authentication, which determines how users are identified and validated before they are allowed access to the system. SQL Server supports two primary authentication modes: Windows authentication and mixed-mode authentication. Windows authentication is the preferred method because it integrates with the underlying Windows operating system, allowing users to authenticate using their Active Directory credentials. This method ensures that user credentials are managed by Windows, which provides a high level of security. With Windows authentication, SQL Server relies on the security policies set by the operating system, such as password complexity requirements and lockout policies.

Mixed-mode authentication, on the other hand, allows SQL Server to use both Windows authentication and SQL Server authentication. SQL Server authentication requires users to provide a username and password that are stored within SQL Server itself. While mixed-mode authentication may be necessary in certain scenarios, such as when connecting from environments that do not support Windows authentication, it is generally considered less secure because the database engine is responsible for managing passwords, which could potentially be compromised. When using mixed-mode authentication, administrators should implement additional security measures, such as strong password policies and the use of complex passwords for SQL Server logins.

Once a user has been authenticated, the next layer of security involves authorization, which determines what actions a user can perform on the SQL Server instance and its databases. SQL Server uses a system of logins, roles, and permissions to control access to resources. A login is an identity that allows a user to connect to the SQL Server instance.

Logins can be mapped to Windows user accounts or groups, or they can be created within SQL Server itself. Once a user has a login, administrators assign them to specific roles that define the actions they are allowed to perform.

SQL Server roles are grouped into two categories: fixed server roles and fixed database roles. Fixed server roles control access to server-level actions, such as managing backups or configuring security settings. For example, the sysadmin role is the highest level of server access, granting full control over all aspects of the SQL Server instance. Database roles, on the other hand, control access to database-specific tasks, such as reading or modifying data within a database. The db_owner role, for example, allows a user to perform all actions within a database, including schema modification and object creation. In addition to fixed roles, SQL Server also allows administrators to create custom roles to suit the specific needs of the organization.

Permissions in SQL Server can be granted at various levels, such as server, database, schema, and object levels. Permissions determine the specific actions that users or roles can perform, such as selecting data from a table, updating records, or executing stored procedures. For example, the SELECT permission allows a user to retrieve data from a table, while the UPDATE permission allows them to modify existing data. Permissions can be granted directly to users or roles, and they can be revoked or denied when necessary. Administrators should always adhere to the principle of least privilege, granting users only the permissions necessary for them to perform their job functions, and regularly reviewing permissions to ensure that they are not overly permissive.

SQL Server also supports a range of encryption features that help protect sensitive data both at rest and in transit. Encryption ensures that even if unauthorized individuals gain access to the data, they will not be able to read it without the proper decryption keys. Transparent Data Encryption (TDE) is one of the most commonly used encryption features in SQL Server. TDE encrypts the entire database, including data files, log files, and backups, without requiring changes to the application. This provides an additional layer of protection for data stored on disk. TDE helps mitigate the risk of data breaches caused by theft of physical storage media, such as hard drives or backup tapes, by making the data unreadable without the appropriate encryption keys.

In addition to TDE, SQL Server supports column-level encryption, which allows administrators to encrypt specific columns in a database. Column-level encryption is particularly useful when dealing with highly sensitive data, such as credit card numbers or personal identification information. Administrators can define which columns should be encrypted and apply encryption at the application or database level. However, while column-level encryption provides a fine-grained approach to data protection, it introduces some performance overhead, as data must be encrypted and decrypted during read and write operations.

SQL Server also supports encryption for data in transit using Secure Sockets Layer (SSL) or Transport Layer Security (TLS). These protocols provide secure communication channels between clients and the SQL Server instance, ensuring that data transmitted over the network is protected from interception. To enable SSL or TLS encryption, administrators must configure both the SQL Server instance and the client application to support these protocols. This is particularly important in scenarios where SQL Server is accessed remotely or across untrusted networks, such as the internet or public cloud environments.

Auditing is another critical aspect of SQL Server security. Auditing allows administrators to track and log user activity, providing visibility into who accessed the system, what actions they performed, and when those actions occurred. SQL Server provides a built-in auditing feature that can capture a wide range of events, such as login attempts, schema changes, and data modifications. SQL Server Audit can be configured to track events at the server or database level, and the resulting audit logs can be stored in a file, the Windows Event Log, or the SQL Server log.

In addition to the built-in auditing capabilities, SQL Server also integrates with third-party security solutions that provide more advanced auditing and compliance features. Regular auditing helps detect suspicious activity, such as unauthorized access attempts or attempts to escalate privileges, and it can also assist in meeting regulatory compliance requirements. SQL Server's auditing features can be tailored to track specific events based on business requirements and security policies.

One of the key best practices in SQL Server security is regular patching and updating of the SQL Server instance. Security vulnerabilities are regularly discovered in software, and applying patches helps protect SQL Server from known exploits. Administrators should monitor for SQL Server updates and apply patches promptly to ensure that the instance remains secure. In addition to patching, SQL Server should be configured with the appropriate security settings, such as disabling unused features and services, enforcing strong authentication policies, and ensuring that firewalls and other perimeter security measures are in place.

SQL Server security is an ongoing process that requires careful planning, implementation, and monitoring. By leveraging SQL Server's authentication, authorization, encryption, and auditing features, administrators can protect sensitive data, prevent unauthorized access, and ensure that the database environment meets organizational security requirements. Additionally, adhering to best practices such as applying patches, managing user permissions, and enforcing strong security policies helps ensure that SQL Server remains secure in the face of evolving threats. Security is not a one-time task but a continuous effort to protect the integrity and confidentiality of data.

# Implementing Authentication and Authorization

Authentication and authorization are two critical pillars of security in SQL Server. Authentication is the process of verifying the identity of a user or system, while authorization determines the permissions or actions that authenticated users are allowed to perform on the system. Properly implementing both authentication and authorization ensures that SQL Server resources are protected from unauthorized access, while also ensuring that users have the appropriate level of access to perform their jobs. This chapter will explore the key concepts behind

SQL Server authentication and authorization, detailing how they work and how to implement them effectively.

Authentication in SQL Server is the process by which a user or application is verified before being granted access to a SQL Server instance. SQL Server supports two main authentication modes: Windows authentication and mixed-mode authentication. Windows authentication is the preferred and most secure method because it uses the security mechanisms of the Windows operating system to authenticate users. With Windows authentication, SQL Server relies on the Active Directory (AD) system to validate a user's credentials, ensuring that users are authenticated based on their existing domain credentials. This integration allows for centralized user management, where users and groups are maintained within Active Directory, simplifying user administration across multiple systems.

One of the key advantages of Windows authentication is that passwords and other sensitive information are never stored within SQL Server. Instead, the operating system manages the user credentials, leveraging features like Kerberos for secure authentication. This reduces the risk of passwords being exposed or compromised and minimizes the administrative burden associated with managing authentication directly within SQL Server. Windows authentication is tightly integrated with the domain security model, and administrators can leverage group memberships and policies set in Active Directory to control access to SQL Server instances.

On the other hand, mixed-mode authentication allows SQL Server to accept both Windows authentication and SQL Server authentication. In mixed-mode authentication, SQL Server manages its own set of logins, separate from Windows accounts. This means users must provide a username and password that are stored within SQL Server, and the authentication process occurs within SQL Server itself. Although mixed-mode authentication is less secure compared to Windows authentication, it is often necessary in certain scenarios where applications or users cannot authenticate using Windows credentials, such as when connecting from non-Windows systems or environments where Windows authentication is not feasible. However, when using mixed-mode authentication, it is essential to enforce strong password policies and limit the use of SQL Server logins to reduce the risk of unauthorized access.

Once a user is authenticated, the next critical step is authorization, which governs what actions an authenticated user can perform on the SQL Server instance. SQL Server uses a combination of logins, roles, and permissions to define and manage access control. A login is an identity that allows a user to connect to the SQL Server instance. Logins are created either from Windows accounts or groups, or they can be specific to SQL Server, created and managed within the database system. When a login is created, administrators can assign the login to various roles, which determine what actions the user is allowed to perform.

SQL Server defines two primary categories of roles: server roles and database roles. Server roles control access to the SQL Server instance itself, allowing administrators to assign broad privileges that apply at the instance level. For example, the sysadmin role is the highest level of server access, granting full control over all aspects of the SQL Server instance. Other fixed server roles include the securityadmin role, which allows for the management of security-related tasks like managing logins and roles, and the dbcreator role, which allows the creation and modification of databases. These fixed server roles provide a predefined set of permissions that can be assigned to logins based on the user's needs.

In addition to server roles, SQL Server also supports database roles, which control access at the database level. Each database can have its own set of roles that define what actions a user can perform within that particular database. For instance, the db_owner role grants a user full control over a specific database, while the db_datareader role allows a user to read data from all tables within a database, and the db_datawriter role allows data modification within the database. Database roles can also be customized by creating user-defined roles, enabling administrators to fine-tune access based on specific business requirements.

Permissions are another key component of SQL Server authorization. Permissions define the specific actions a user can perform on objects within a database, such as reading or modifying data, executing stored procedures, or managing database schemas. Permissions can be granted at various levels, such as server, database, schema, or object levels. For example, granting the SELECT permission on a table allows a user to retrieve data from the table, while granting the INSERT permission allows them to add new rows. Permissions are granted directly to logins or database roles, and administrators can use the GRANT, DENY, and REVOKE commands to control access to various SQL Server resources.

One of the most important best practices when implementing authorization in SQL Server is the principle of least privilege. This principle dictates that users should be granted the minimum level of access necessary for them to perform their job functions. By limiting the scope of user permissions, administrators can reduce the potential for accidental or malicious actions that could compromise data integrity, availability, or confidentiality. Over-permissioned users may have access to sensitive data or administrative tasks that are outside the scope of their responsibilities, leading to potential security risks. Regularly reviewing user roles and permissions helps ensure that users do not retain unnecessary access rights after changes in their job roles or responsibilities.

SQL Server also provides mechanisms for managing user access across multiple databases within the same instance. By using contained databases, administrators can isolate database-specific users from the instance-level security model, enabling users to authenticate and access only the databases they are explicitly authorized to use. Contained databases simplify user management, particularly in scenarios where a database is being moved across instances or when working in cloud environments. Additionally, SQL Server allows for the creation of schema-based security models, where users are granted permissions on database objects within a specific schema, rather than granting permissions directly on individual objects.

Another important consideration for SQL Server authentication and authorization is auditing and monitoring user activity. SQL Server provides tools to monitor who is accessing the system and what actions they are performing. Auditing helps ensure compliance with security policies and provides a mechanism to detect and respond to suspicious activity. SQL Server's built-in audit functionality allows administrators to track events such as successful and failed login attempts, data modifications, and changes to security settings. Auditing can be configured at both the server and database levels to capture relevant security events. Logs generated by SQL Server audits can be reviewed to investigate potential security breaches or unauthorized access attempts.

In addition to SQL Server's native auditing features, third-party security solutions can be integrated to provide more advanced logging and monitoring capabilities. These solutions often provide real-time alerts, comprehensive reporting, and advanced analytics to detect anomalies and potential threats more effectively. Organizations subject to regulatory compliance requirements, such as those in healthcare or finance, often leverage these tools to maintain audit trails and demonstrate adherence to data protection standards.

Implementing robust authentication and authorization mechanisms is essential for ensuring the security of SQL Server environments. By leveraging Windows authentication, using appropriate server and database roles, and following the principle of least privilege, database administrators can protect data from unauthorized access and ensure that users have access only to the resources they need. Furthermore, by incorporating auditing and monitoring practices, administrators can track and respond to security threats, maintaining the integrity and confidentiality of sensitive information. Properly implemented authentication and authorization form the foundation of a secure SQL Server environment, helping organizations safeguard their data and meet security and compliance requirements.

# SQL Server Encryption Techniques

Encryption is one of the most essential techniques for safeguarding sensitive data within a SQL Server environment. In a world where data breaches and unauthorized access are persistent threats, protecting data through encryption ensures its confidentiality, integrity, and availability, even in the event of theft or unauthorized access. SQL Server provides a robust set of encryption features to help administrators secure data both at rest and in transit. Understanding how these encryption techniques work, when to implement them, and the best practices for their use is critical for building a secure database environment. This chapter will explore the encryption techniques available in SQL Server, including Transparent Data Encryption (TDE), column-level encryption, Always Encrypted, and encryption for data in transit.

Transparent Data Encryption (TDE) is one of the most widely used encryption techniques in SQL Server. TDE provides real-time encryption of an entire database, ensuring that all data, including data files, log files, and backup files, are encrypted. The key feature of TDE is that it encrypts data without requiring changes to the application. This means that the encryption process is transparent to users and applications, allowing them to continue interacting with the database without needing to be aware of the encryption. TDE uses the database's encryption key to encrypt and decrypt data on the fly as it is read from or written to the disk. This makes it particularly useful for protecting data at rest, especially for preventing unauthorized access to the underlying storage media in case of physical theft of the server or backup devices.

TDE operates by utilizing a layered encryption model. The database encryption key (DEK) is used to encrypt the data within the database files, while a certificate or asymmetric key is used to protect the DEK itself. This hierarchical key structure ensures that the DEK can be securely stored and managed, while also allowing for the encryption and decryption processes to remain efficient. TDE does not require changes to the application or the database schema, making it an attractive option for encrypting entire databases with minimal disruption to operations. However, while TDE encrypts data at rest, it does not provide encryption for data while it is being transmitted across the network, which is where other encryption techniques come into play.

Another important feature of SQL Server encryption is column-level encryption. This method allows administrators to encrypt specific columns in a database rather than the entire database. Column-level encryption is particularly useful when dealing with highly sensitive data, such as credit card numbers, personal identification numbers, or social security numbers, which must be protected due to regulatory requirements. By encrypting specific columns, administrators can reduce the performance overhead associated with full database encryption, as only the encrypted columns require additional processing during data access. SQL Server supports both symmetric and asymmetric encryption algorithms for column-level encryption. Symmetric encryption, such as the AES (Advanced Encryption Standard) algorithm, is commonly used for column-level encryption because it is faster and more efficient than asymmetric encryption, which uses a pair of public and private keys.

When using column-level encryption, the encryption and decryption operations are typically performed within the application or database queries. This means that the application must be aware of the encryption and decryption process and be responsible for passing the appropriate keys to SQL Server to decrypt the data. One of the challenges of column-level encryption is key management. Because each column is encrypted with a specific key, securely storing and distributing those keys is critical to maintaining the integrity of the encryption process. SQL Server provides several features for key management, including the use of the SQL Server Certificate Store and the Key Management Service, which help administrators store and manage encryption keys in a secure manner.

Always Encrypted is another powerful encryption feature in SQL Server that provides end-to-end encryption for sensitive data. Unlike TDE or column-level encryption, Always Encrypted ensures that data is encrypted both at rest and in transit, and it is never decrypted outside of the client application. This means that even SQL Server administrators do not have access to the decrypted data, providing an additional layer of security for highly sensitive information. Always Encrypted uses two types of keys: a column encryption key (CEK) and a master key. The CEK is used to encrypt and decrypt data, while the master key is used to protect the CEK. The encryption and decryption operations are handled by the client application, which communicates directly with SQL Server. This ensures that the data is encrypted on the client side before being sent to the database and remains encrypted throughout the entire lifecycle.

Always Encrypted is particularly useful for scenarios where sensitive data must be protected from unauthorized access by both database administrators and other users who may have access to the database itself. This makes it an ideal solution for applications that handle personally identifiable information (PII), healthcare data, or financial records. One of the main benefits of Always Encrypted is that it allows the database to perform its normal operations, such as query execution and indexing, without ever accessing the decrypted data. However, Always Encrypted does introduce some performance overhead, as the encryption and decryption processes must be performed by the client application. Furthermore, it is important to note that not all SQL Server operations can work with Always Encrypted columns, such as certain types of indexing and querying that require access to the plaintext values.

In addition to these encryption techniques for securing data at rest, SQL Server also provides encryption for data in transit. SQL Server supports Secure Sockets Layer (SSL) and Transport Layer Security (TLS) protocols to encrypt data as it travels across the network. This encryption ensures that sensitive data, such as login credentials and query results, is protected from interception or tampering during transmission. SSL and TLS protocols provide a secure communication channel between SQL Server clients and the database server, making it difficult for attackers to eavesdrop on the communication. SQL Server can be configured to require encryption for all connections, ensuring that all data transmitted between clients and servers is encrypted.

To enable encryption for data in transit, administrators must configure SQL Server to use SSL or TLS certificates. These certificates are used to authenticate the server and establish a secure communication channel. SQL Server supports both server-side and client-side certificates, which allow for mutual authentication between the client and server. It is important to regularly update and manage these certificates to maintain a high level of security. Additionally, administrators should consider enforcing encryption for all client connections, especially when connecting over untrusted networks, such as the internet or public cloud environments.

Key management is one of the most critical aspects of implementing encryption in SQL Server. Whether using TDE, column-level encryption, Always Encrypted, or encryption for data in transit, the management of encryption keys must be handled with care. SQL Server provides a variety of tools and features to manage encryption keys, such as the SQL Server Certificate Store, the Database Master Key (DMK), and the Extensible Key Management (EKM) feature, which allows SQL Server to integrate with third-party key management systems. Proper key management ensures that keys are securely stored, rotated, and audited, reducing the risk of unauthorized access to encrypted data.

Implementing encryption in SQL Server is essential for organizations that need to protect sensitive data from unauthorized access or breaches. SQL Server provides a range of encryption techniques that can be tailored to meet the needs of different data protection scenarios. By using techniques such as Transparent Data Encryption, column-level encryption, Always Encrypted, and SSL/TLS encryption for data in transit, administrators can build a secure environment that protects data at every stage of its lifecycle. However, it is important to understand the performance trade-offs and key management requirements associated with each encryption method and to implement encryption in a way that aligns with the organization's security policies and regulatory requirements.

# Managing and Auditing SQL Server Permissions

Managing and auditing SQL Server permissions is a vital component of maintaining a secure and efficient database environment. Permissions control who can access SQL Server resources and what actions they can perform, such as reading data, modifying records, or managing the database schema. Properly managing permissions ensures that users have access only to the resources they need to perform their job functions, which minimizes the risk of unauthorized access, data breaches, and other security threats. Additionally, auditing permissions provides a way to track user activity, monitor compliance, and detect potential security violations. This chapter will explore the principles of SQL Server permissions management, best practices for implementing them, and the tools available for auditing permissions.

Permissions in SQL Server are used to control access to various types of objects, including databases, tables, views, stored procedures, and more. These permissions are granted to users and roles, allowing them to perform specific actions on the objects. Permissions can be granted at different levels, from the server level, which controls access to the entire SQL Server instance, to the object level, which controls access to individual tables or views within a database. The flexibility of SQL Server's permission model allows administrators to create fine-grained access controls that can be tailored to the needs of the organization.

At the core of SQL Server's permission system are logins and roles. A login is an identity used to connect to the SQL Server instance, and it can be mapped to a Windows user or group, or it can be a SQL Server-specific login. Once a login is created, it is assigned to one or more roles, which define the actions the user is allowed to perform. Roles are categorized into server roles, which control access to server-level actions, and database roles, which control access to database-specific actions. For example, the sysadmin server role allows full control over all SQL Server operations, while the db_owner database role allows full control over a specific database. SQL Server also provides user-defined roles, which enable administrators to create custom roles tailored to specific business requirements.

Once roles have been assigned, permissions are granted to those roles to allow specific actions on SQL Server objects. Permissions can be granted directly to a user or to a role. When permissions are granted to a role, all members of that role inherit the permissions. Permissions are specific to the type of object being accessed, and the actions allowed by each permission vary. For example, the SELECT permission allows a user to read data from a table, while the INSERT permission allows them to add new data. Permissions can also be granted for more complex actions, such as executing stored procedures or managing indexes. It is important to grant permissions based on the principle of least privilege, meaning that users should only be granted the minimum level of access required for their tasks.

SQL Server allows administrators to further refine permission management by using schemas. A schema is a container for database objects, such as tables and views, and permissions can be granted on a schema level, rather than on individual objects. This simplifies permission management by allowing administrators to group related objects together and control access to the entire group of objects. For example, an administrator can create a schema for customer data and grant a specific role permission to access all tables and views within that schema, without needing to grant permissions to each object individually.

Managing SQL Server permissions also involves controlling the propagation of permissions. SQL Server allows administrators to grant, deny, and revoke permissions, and it is essential to understand how these operations work. When a permission is granted to a user or role, it allows them to perform the specified action. However, if a permission is denied, it overrides any previously granted permissions for that action, regardless of whether the permission was granted directly or through a role. Denying permissions is a powerful tool for restricting access, but it should be used with caution, as it can create unexpected results if not carefully managed. Revoke, on the other hand, removes a permission, but it does not override previously granted permissions. Revoke is generally used to remove unnecessary permissions, while deny is used to explicitly block access.

One of the challenges of managing SQL Server permissions is ensuring that permissions are not overly permissive. Over-permissioning occurs when users are granted more access than they need, potentially exposing sensitive data or allowing users to perform actions they should not be allowed to do. Over-permissioning can result from poorly defined roles, granting excessive privileges, or not reviewing permissions regularly. To avoid this, administrators should regularly audit permissions to ensure that users and roles have only the permissions they need. Additionally, permission management tools, such as SQL Server Management Studio (SSMS), can be used to automate and streamline the process of assigning and reviewing permissions.

Auditing SQL Server permissions is an essential part of ensuring that access controls are being followed and that the database environment is secure. Auditing allows administrators to track who is accessing the system, what actions they are performing, and whether any unauthorized actions are taking place. SQL Server provides a built-in auditing feature that allows administrators to capture a wide range of events, such as login attempts, data modifications, and changes to security settings. The SQL Server Audit feature captures these events and stores them in audit logs, which can be reviewed to identify potential security violations or compliance issues.

SQL Server Audit can be configured to capture events at the server or database level, and the resulting audit logs can be stored in various locations, including a file, the Windows Event Log, or the SQL Server log. Auditing can be configured to track specific actions, such as failed login attempts, changes to permissions, or execution of specific queries. This provides administrators with visibility into user activity, allowing them to identify suspicious behavior or violations of organizational security policies. Auditing can also help organizations meet regulatory compliance requirements, such as those set forth by the GDPR or HIPAA, by providing a mechanism to track and report on access to sensitive data.

In addition to the native auditing capabilities of SQL Server, third-party security solutions can be integrated to provide more advanced auditing and monitoring features. These tools often include real-time alerts, detailed reporting, and more sophisticated analysis of audit data. They can be used to detect unusual patterns of activity, such as unauthorized access to sensitive data or attempts to escalate privileges, and provide administrators with the information needed to respond quickly to potential threats.

Regularly reviewing and auditing permissions is essential for maintaining a secure SQL Server environment. This involves not only reviewing the permissions granted to individual users but also auditing role memberships, examining schema-based access controls, and ensuring that permissions are consistent with the principle of least privilege. By auditing permissions and monitoring user activity, administrators can identify and mitigate potential security risks before they become significant issues.

Effective permission management and auditing are critical to the security of a SQL Server environment. By carefully controlling who has access to what data and actions, and regularly reviewing and auditing these permissions, administrators can ensure that only authorized users are granted access to sensitive information. Implementing strong permission management practices and auditing controls reduces the risk of unauthorized access, data breaches, and non-compliance, helping to maintain the integrity and confidentiality of the database system.

# Advanced SQL Server Security Features

SQL Server provides a range of security features to protect databases, ensure compliance with regulatory standards, and safeguard data from unauthorized access. While basic security measures such as authentication and access control are essential, advanced security features enable administrators to go beyond the fundamentals and add additional layers of protection. These advanced features are designed to address the evolving landscape of database security, where threats are increasingly sophisticated and data is often under constant scrutiny. This chapter will explore some of the advanced security features available in SQL Server, including encryption, dynamic data masking, row-level security, SQL Server auditing, and more.

One of the most important advanced security features in SQL Server is encryption. SQL Server provides multiple encryption techniques to protect data both at rest and in transit. Transparent Data Encryption (TDE) is one of the most widely used encryption methods. It encrypts the entire database, including data files, log files, and backup files, ensuring that all data stored on disk is protected from unauthorized access. TDE operates transparently, meaning that users and applications can continue to access the data without needing to be aware of the encryption process. This makes TDE an excellent choice for securing databases in production environments, where encryption should not impact application performance or require changes to the application code.

In addition to TDE, SQL Server also supports column-level encryption, which allows administrators to encrypt individual columns within a table. This is particularly useful for protecting sensitive information such as credit card numbers, social security numbers, or personal health information. Column-level encryption can be implemented using either symmetric or asymmetric encryption algorithms.

Symmetric encryption is often preferred for performance reasons, as it is faster than asymmetric encryption, but both options provide strong protection for sensitive data. One challenge with column-level encryption is managing the encryption keys securely, as the encryption and decryption process requires access to these keys.

Always Encrypted is another advanced encryption feature in SQL Server that provides end-to-end encryption of sensitive data. Unlike TDE and column-level encryption, Always Encrypted ensures that data is encrypted before it reaches the SQL Server instance and is never decrypted on the server side. This means that even database administrators and other users with access to the server cannot view the sensitive data. The encryption and decryption processes are handled by the client application, which encrypts data before sending it to the server and decrypts data when it is retrieved. Always Encrypted uses two types of keys: a column encryption key (CEK) and a master key, providing a secure method for storing and managing these keys. This feature is particularly useful for protecting data that needs to remain confidential, even from those who manage the database infrastructure.

Dynamic Data Masking is another advanced security feature in SQL Server that helps protect sensitive data by obscuring it for non-privileged users. With dynamic data masking, administrators can define masking rules on columns that store sensitive information, such as credit card numbers or email addresses. When a non-privileged user queries the data, the masked values are returned instead of the actual data. For example, a credit card number might appear as "****-1234" to a non-privileged user, while the full number remains visible to authorized users with higher privileges. This feature is useful in scenarios where users need to access certain data but should not be able to see the complete details. Dynamic Data Masking does not alter the underlying data and can be applied without changing the application code.

Row-Level Security (RLS) is another powerful feature that allows administrators to control access to rows in a table based on the characteristics of the user executing the query. RLS enables fine-grained access control, where users can only see the rows that are relevant to them. For example, in a sales application, a sales representative might only be able to view customer records associated with their specific territory. RLS works by creating a security policy that is applied to tables, and using predicates to filter the data based on user identity or session context. This ensures that each user only sees the data they are authorized to access, providing an additional layer of security for sensitive data within a single table.

SQL Server also provides advanced auditing capabilities, which are essential for tracking user activity and ensuring compliance with security policies. The SQL Server Audit feature enables administrators to track events such as login attempts, database access, and changes to database objects. Auditing is a critical part of a comprehensive security strategy, as it provides visibility into who is accessing the system, what actions they are performing, and whether any unauthorized activities are occurring. SQL Server Audit can be configured to capture specific actions, such as changes to security settings or access to sensitive data, and the resulting audit logs can be stored in a file, Windows Event Log, or SQL Server log. By regularly reviewing audit logs, administrators can detect potential security breaches, investigate suspicious activities, and ensure compliance with regulatory requirements such as GDPR or HIPAA.

SQL Server also supports fine-grained access control through the use of security principals, which can be used to define who has access to specific database resources and what actions they can perform. Principals in SQL Server include logins, users, and roles, and they are used to assign permissions on a server or database level. Server roles define access to server-level operations, such as managing backups or configuring security settings, while database roles define access to database-level resources, such as tables, views, and stored procedures. By carefully managing roles and permissions, administrators can ensure that users have access only to the data and operations necessary for their roles, reducing the risk of unauthorized access or data breaches.

Another advanced security feature in SQL Server is the ability to implement fine-grained password policies and multi-factor authentication (MFA). SQL Server allows administrators to enforce strong password policies for SQL Server logins, ensuring that passwords meet complexity requirements, such as a minimum length, the use of uppercase and lowercase letters, and the inclusion of special characters. Additionally, multi-factor authentication can be implemented to add an extra layer of security for user logins. With MFA, users are required to provide additional verification, such as a one-time passcode sent to their mobile device, in addition to their password. This greatly enhances the security of user authentication, particularly in environments where sensitive data is being accessed.

SQL Server also integrates with Active Directory (AD) to provide centralized identity management and further enhance security. By using Windows Authentication, administrators can leverage Active Directory to manage user accounts and groups, enforce group policies, and control access to SQL Server instances based on Windows security settings. This integration simplifies user management, as credentials are stored and managed centrally in Active Directory, and users can authenticate using their existing Windows accounts.

SQL Server's advanced security features provide a comprehensive suite of tools to protect sensitive data and ensure compliance with security standards. Encryption techniques like TDE, column-level encryption, and Always Encrypted provide robust protection for data at rest and in transit, while features like Dynamic Data Masking, Row-Level Security, and auditing offer fine-grained control over who can access data and what actions they can perform. By combining these advanced features with best practices for role-based access control and secure authentication, administrators can create a SQL Server environment that is resilient against a wide range of security threats. As the threat landscape continues to evolve, these advanced security features will play an increasingly critical role in securing SQL Server environments and protecting sensitive data.

# Optimizing SQL Server for High Availability

High availability (HA) is a critical requirement for SQL Server environments, particularly for businesses and applications that rely on continuous access to data. In today's highly competitive and data-driven world, even small periods of downtime can result in significant operational disruption, lost revenue, and diminished customer trust.

Optimizing SQL Server for high availability ensures that database services remain operational and accessible, even in the face of hardware failures, network issues, or other unexpected events. Achieving high availability involves a combination of hardware, software, and configuration strategies designed to minimize downtime, provide redundancy, and ensure that data remains consistent and accessible at all times. This chapter will explore various techniques and best practices for optimizing SQL Server to meet high availability requirements, focusing on key features such as AlwaysOn Availability Groups, database mirroring, log shipping, clustering, and other fault-tolerant solutions.

One of the most widely used solutions for high availability in SQL Server is the AlwaysOn Availability Groups feature, introduced in SQL Server 2012. AlwaysOn Availability Groups enable high availability by replicating databases across multiple instances of SQL Server, ensuring that a copy of the database is always available on another server in the event of a failure. With AlwaysOn, a primary replica holds the read-write copy of the database, while one or more secondary replicas contain read-only copies. These replicas can be located on different servers, providing redundancy and minimizing the impact of hardware or network failures. If the primary replica becomes unavailable, the system can automatically failover to one of the secondary replicas, ensuring that database services remain operational.

AlwaysOn Availability Groups can be configured in two primary modes: synchronous and asynchronous. In synchronous mode, transactions are committed to both the primary and secondary replicas simultaneously, ensuring that both copies are always in sync. This provides high data consistency but can introduce latency due to the need for both replicas to acknowledge each transaction before it is committed. Asynchronous mode, on the other hand, allows the primary replica to commit transactions without waiting for the secondary replica to acknowledge them. While this improves performance and reduces latency, it introduces a small risk of data loss if a failover occurs before the secondary replica has caught up with the primary. The choice between synchronous and asynchronous modes depends on the specific requirements of the application, with synchronous mode being preferred for mission-critical applications where data loss is unacceptable.

Another high availability solution is SQL Server's database mirroring feature, which provides database redundancy by maintaining two copies of a database—one on the primary server and one on a mirrored server. Like AlwaysOn, database mirroring ensures that if the primary server becomes unavailable, the mirrored server can take over, allowing the database to remain accessible. SQL Server database mirroring operates in two modes: high safety and high performance. In high safety mode, transactions are fully committed to both the primary and mirrored databases, ensuring data consistency but introducing a slight performance overhead due to the need for transaction synchronization. In high performance mode, transactions are committed only to the primary database, with changes being sent asynchronously to the mirror, which reduces performance impact but can result in data loss during a failover event.

Database mirroring was a widely used feature in previous versions of SQL Server, but it has been largely superseded by AlwaysOn Availability Groups in recent versions. Nonetheless, database mirroring can still be a valuable solution in certain scenarios, particularly when only a single database needs to be mirrored, and the failover process is relatively simple. It is important to note that database mirroring requires a dedicated SQL Server instance for the mirrored database, making it more resource-intensive compared to AlwaysOn, which allows for multiple databases to be included in a single availability group.

Log shipping is another method for optimizing SQL Server for high availability. In a log shipping configuration, the transaction log from the primary database is periodically backed up, transferred to a secondary server, and applied to a copy of the database. This process ensures that the secondary database is kept up to date with the primary database, and in the event of a failure, the secondary database can be brought online quickly by applying the latest transaction logs. Log shipping is often used in conjunction with other high availability solutions, such as database mirroring or clustering, to provide an additional layer of redundancy and disaster recovery.

Log shipping is relatively simple to configure and maintain compared to AlwaysOn or database mirroring, but it does not offer the same level of near-real-time failover capabilities. Log shipping is typically used in scenarios where occasional failover is acceptable, such as in disaster recovery configurations or for workloads that do not require the highest levels of availability. One drawback of log shipping is the potential for data loss during a failover event, as the secondary database may not be fully up to date with the primary database at the time of failure.

SQL Server clustering is another important feature for high availability, providing failover protection at the server level rather than at the database level. SQL Server failover clustering involves grouping multiple physical servers into a cluster, with one server acting as the primary node and others as secondary nodes. The primary node holds the active instance of SQL Server and provides database services, while the secondary nodes are available to take over in the event of a failure. When a failover occurs, the active SQL Server instance is automatically moved to one of the secondary nodes, minimizing downtime and maintaining access to the databases.

Failover clustering provides a high level of availability by protecting the entire SQL Server instance, including all databases, configurations, and settings. This differs from AlwaysOn and database mirroring, which focus primarily on protecting individual databases. Failover clustering also requires shared storage, such as a Storage Area Network (SAN), to ensure that all nodes in the cluster can access the same database files. While clustering provides a robust solution for high availability, it can be more complex and expensive to implement and manage, especially in large-scale environments with multiple SQL Server instances.

In addition to these primary high availability solutions, administrators must also consider other factors that contribute to overall system availability. These include monitoring SQL Server health and performance, implementing robust backup and recovery strategies, and ensuring that hardware infrastructure is properly configured for redundancy. Regular monitoring of SQL Server instances, using tools like SQL Server Management Studio (SSMS) and third-party monitoring solutions, helps administrators identify potential issues before they lead to downtime. Similarly, a comprehensive backup strategy, including regular full and transaction log backups, is essential for ensuring that data can be quickly restored in the event of a failure.

For businesses that require continuous availability, SQL Server offers a wide range of high availability solutions that can be tailored to meet the specific needs of the organization. Whether using AlwaysOn Availability Groups, database mirroring, log shipping, or clustering, the goal is to ensure that SQL Server databases are always accessible, even in the event of hardware failures, network disruptions, or other unexpected incidents. Properly optimizing SQL Server for high availability involves understanding the strengths and limitations of each solution and selecting the most appropriate option based on business requirements, performance considerations, and budget constraints. Through careful planning and implementation, SQL Server can be configured to deliver maximum uptime and reliability for critical business applications.

# Implementing and Managing SQL Server Clustering

SQL Server clustering is a robust solution designed to ensure high availability for critical database applications. It allows multiple servers, or nodes, to work together to provide a fault-tolerant environment that minimizes downtime and ensures that the database remains operational, even in the event of hardware failures or other disruptions. The primary goal of SQL Server clustering is to provide automatic failover, where another server node can take over if the primary server fails, ensuring continuous service without manual intervention. This chapter will explore the process of implementing and managing SQL Server clustering, highlighting key concepts, configuration steps, and best practices for ensuring optimal performance and reliability.

SQL Server clustering, often referred to as SQL Server failover clustering, is based on the Windows Server Failover Clustering (WSFC) feature, which allows multiple physical servers to form a cluster. Each node in the cluster is a separate physical machine, but they all share access to the same storage system, typically a shared Storage Area Network (SAN) or shared disk. The shared storage is crucial because it ensures that all nodes in the cluster can access the same data files, transaction logs, and other SQL Server resources. This shared storage setup is what enables failover, as all nodes in the cluster are essentially working with the same data, allowing a failed node to be quickly replaced by another node in the cluster without data loss.

The first step in implementing SQL Server clustering is setting up the Windows Server Failover Cluster (WSFC). This involves installing the failover clustering feature on each node and ensuring that the nodes are networked together and can communicate effectively. During the setup of WSFC, administrators must define cluster roles, such as the SQL Server instance, and configure the cluster's shared storage. This shared storage is typically implemented through a SAN, but it can also be configured using Storage Spaces Direct or other similar technologies. The configuration of shared storage is critical because SQL Server clustering requires all nodes to access the same storage in a manner that is consistent and highly available.

Once the Windows Server Failover Cluster is set up, the next step is to install SQL Server on the cluster nodes. SQL Server clustering requires a specialized installation process, different from a standard SQL Server installation. During the installation, SQL Server is installed as a clustered instance, which means the SQL Server instance will be able to run on any node in the cluster. A clustered SQL Server instance requires a virtual network name (VNN) and a virtual IP address (VIP), which allow clients to connect to the SQL Server instance through a single, consistent name and IP address, even if the instance fails over to a different node in the cluster. This ensures that client applications do not need to be reconfigured during a failover, simplifying the process of maintaining high availability.

One of the most important features of SQL Server clustering is its ability to provide automatic failover. When a failure occurs on the primary node, whether due to hardware failure, network issues, or any other cause, the failover process automatically transfers the SQL Server instance to a secondary node in the cluster. This process is handled by the WSFC, which monitors the health of each node and detects when a node is no longer responsive. Once the failure is detected, the WSFC initiates the failover process, transferring the SQL Server instance to another node with minimal downtime. The failover process includes transferring the virtual network name, virtual IP address, and SQL

Server instance to the new node, ensuring that client applications can reconnect without requiring manual intervention.

SQL Server clustering can be configured with either a single-node or multi-node configuration, depending on the organization's requirements. A single-node cluster setup consists of one active node running SQL Server, with one or more passive nodes that are on standby and can take over in the event of a failure. In a multi-node cluster setup, multiple active nodes can run SQL Server instances simultaneously, distributing the load across multiple machines and improving scalability. The choice of configuration depends on factors such as the desired level of fault tolerance, scalability requirements, and budget constraints.

To ensure that SQL Server clustering operates smoothly, regular monitoring and management are required. SQL Server provides a range of tools and features to help administrators monitor the health and performance of the cluster. SQL Server Management Studio (SSMS) allows administrators to check the status of the SQL Server instance and cluster, monitor resource utilization, and track failover events. In addition, the SQL Server Error Log and Windows Event Log provide critical information about any issues related to the cluster, such as node failures or connectivity problems.

Another important aspect of managing SQL Server clustering is handling backup and disaster recovery. While SQL Server clustering ensures high availability by automatically failing over to a secondary node in the event of a failure, it does not replace the need for a robust backup strategy. Regular backups of databases, transaction logs, and other critical data should be taken to ensure that data can be restored in the event of a major disaster, such as a complete server failure. Additionally, it is important to test the failover and failback processes regularly to ensure that the cluster is functioning as expected and that the SQL Server instance can be quickly restored in the event of a failure.

Performance optimization is another critical aspect of managing SQL Server clustering. While clustering provides fault tolerance and high availability, it is essential to ensure that the cluster is configured to handle the required workload efficiently. This includes optimizing the shared storage configuration to ensure fast access to data, configuring SQL Server instances to distribute the workload evenly across cluster nodes, and monitoring the performance of the cluster using tools such as SQL Server Performance Monitor and Windows Resource Monitor. It is also essential to ensure that the network infrastructure supporting the cluster is configured for high performance and low latency to avoid potential bottlenecks.

SQL Server clustering also provides built-in support for high availability of other services, such as SQL Server Reporting Services (SSRS), SQL Server Integration Services (SSIS), and SQL Server Analysis Services (SSAS). These services can be configured to run in a clustered environment, ensuring that they remain available and operational in the event of a failure. This extends the benefits of clustering beyond the core SQL Server database engine and provides high availability for all critical SQL Server services.

To enhance the effectiveness of SQL Server clustering, administrators should follow best practices for clustering configuration, such as ensuring that each node in the cluster is equipped with identical hardware and running the same version of SQL Server and the operating system. This minimizes the risk of compatibility issues and ensures that failovers occur smoothly. Additionally, it is recommended to implement regular maintenance tasks, such as updating software patches, updating antivirus definitions, and verifying hardware integrity, to prevent potential issues before they lead to downtime.

Implementing and managing SQL Server clustering is a complex but powerful approach to ensuring high availability for SQL Server environments. By leveraging the features of Windows Server Failover Clustering and SQL Server, administrators can create a resilient database environment that can withstand failures and continue to provide uninterrupted service. With careful planning, configuration, and ongoing management, SQL Server clustering provides a reliable solution for businesses that require maximum uptime and minimal disruption to critical data services. Through monitoring, performance optimization, and adherence to best practices, SQL Server clustering can provide a high-availability environment that meets the demands of modern, data-intensive applications.

# Using SQL Server AlwaysOn Availability Groups

SQL Server AlwaysOn Availability Groups (AGs) provide one of the most robust solutions for high availability and disaster recovery in SQL Server environments. AlwaysOn AGs allow for the replication of a SQL Server database across multiple instances, known as replicas, providing both data redundancy and the ability to failover in case of a server or hardware failure. Unlike previous high availability solutions like database mirroring or log shipping, AlwaysOn Availability Groups offer a more flexible, scalable, and efficient way to ensure that critical data remains accessible even during outages. This chapter explores the concepts behind AlwaysOn Availability Groups, how they are implemented, and best practices for leveraging their capabilities in SQL Server environments.

The heart of AlwaysOn Availability Groups lies in the replication of databases between a primary replica and one or more secondary replicas. A primary replica is the main server where read-write operations take place, while the secondary replicas maintain copies of the database that are typically read-only. These secondary replicas are synchronized with the primary replica to ensure that the data is kept up-to-date across all replicas, providing redundancy and fault tolerance. In the event of a failure on the primary replica, the system can automatically failover to one of the secondary replicas, ensuring that database services remain available without significant downtime.

One of the key features of AlwaysOn Availability Groups is that they support multiple databases within a single availability group. This makes them far more flexible than older technologies like database mirroring, which could only protect a single database at a time. By grouping related databases together in an availability group, administrators can simplify management, ensure that all critical databases are protected, and reduce the complexity of failover operations. The AlwaysOn AG feature can protect an entire application's databases, rather than requiring individual configuration for each database. This offers significant advantages in environments where multiple databases need to be kept in sync and highly available.

AlwaysOn Availability Groups operate in two primary modes: synchronous and asynchronous. In synchronous mode, transactions on the primary replica are committed to both the primary and the secondary replicas simultaneously. This ensures that both replicas are in perfect sync, providing high data consistency. This mode is typically used in scenarios where data loss is unacceptable, as it guarantees that no committed transaction will be lost, even in the event of a failover. However, the synchronous mode can introduce a small amount of latency, as each transaction must be acknowledged by both the primary and secondary replicas before being committed. This tradeoff in performance is acceptable in environments where data integrity is of utmost importance.

Asynchronous mode, on the other hand, allows transactions to be committed on the primary replica without waiting for the secondary replicas to acknowledge the transaction. While this improves performance by reducing latency, it does introduce the potential for data loss in the event of a failover, as the secondary replica may not have caught up with the primary replica. Asynchronous mode is often used in geographically distributed environments, where replicas are located far apart, and the network latency would be too high for synchronous replication to work efficiently. In such scenarios, the priority is ensuring availability and minimizing latency, even at the cost of some potential data loss.

The configuration of AlwaysOn Availability Groups requires careful planning and consideration. First, the underlying infrastructure must support AlwaysOn AGs, which require Windows Server Failover Clustering (WSFC) as the basis for replication. Each server node in the cluster needs to be part of the same Active Directory domain and must have access to shared storage, although AlwaysOn AGs can also work in environments without shared storage, as long as network connectivity between replicas is stable and reliable. The configuration process also requires configuring a listener, which provides a consistent name and IP address that clients can use to connect to the availability group. This ensures that client applications can connect to the database without needing to know which replica is currently active.

One of the most important aspects of AlwaysOn Availability Groups is its ability to provide automatic failover. When a failure occurs on the primary replica, the system can automatically promote one of the secondary replicas to be the new primary, ensuring minimal downtime and maintaining service availability. Automatic failover is possible only if the availability group is configured with two synchronous replicas. When the failover occurs, the new primary replica takes over the virtual network name and IP address of the failed primary replica, allowing clients to reconnect without requiring manual intervention. This seamless failover process is critical in high-availability environments, as it ensures that users experience little to no disruption in service.

One of the challenges of using AlwaysOn AGs is the management of backups. While AlwaysOn Availability Groups provide excellent high availability, backups still need to be performed regularly to protect against data loss. SQL Server allows backups to be taken from any of the replicas in the availability group, not just the primary replica. However, to prevent any potential issues with backup consistency, it is recommended to perform backups on the primary replica or on a designated backup replica. In a high-availability setup, it is crucial to create a comprehensive backup strategy that includes full, differential, and transaction log backups to ensure that data can be restored in case of a failure or disaster.

Another challenge with AlwaysOn AGs is maintaining performance across replicas. Since secondary replicas are read-only by default, they can be used to offload read workloads, such as reporting queries, from the primary replica. This helps to reduce the load on the primary server and improves overall system performance. However, using secondary replicas for read workloads requires careful monitoring of their synchronization with the primary replica. If the secondary replicas fall too far behind, read queries may return outdated data. To manage this, SQL Server provides tools such as the AlwaysOn dashboard in SQL Server Management Studio (SSMS), which helps administrators monitor the health and performance of the availability group and identify any synchronization issues.

Security is another important consideration when implementing AlwaysOn Availability Groups. SQL Server offers several security features that ensure that data remains protected, even in a multi-replica environment. For example, SQL Server supports encryption of data in transit using SSL/TLS, ensuring that data is encrypted as it moves between replicas. Additionally, AlwaysOn AGs support Transparent Data Encryption (TDE), which encrypts the database files to protect data at rest. By combining these features with role-based access control (RBAC) and Windows authentication, administrators can ensure that only authorized users and applications can access the data within the availability group.

Monitoring and maintenance are critical for the ongoing success of AlwaysOn Availability Groups. Administrators should regularly review the health of the availability group, monitor the status of replicas, and check for any issues that could affect performance or availability. SQL Server provides several monitoring tools, including the AlwaysOn dashboard in SSMS and dynamic management views (DMVs), which provide real-time insights into the status of the availability group, replicas, and data synchronization. Regular testing of failover processes is also essential to ensure that the system can recover smoothly in the event of a failure.

SQL Server AlwaysOn Availability Groups offer a powerful, flexible solution for ensuring high availability and disaster recovery in SQL Server environments. By providing multiple replicas, automatic failover, and support for both synchronous and asynchronous replication, AlwaysOn AGs can meet the needs of both small and large organizations with varying performance and availability requirements. While implementing AlwaysOn AGs requires careful configuration and planning, it offers significant benefits in terms of fault tolerance, scalability, and improved performance. By combining AlwaysOn with other SQL Server features such as encryption, backup strategies, and performance tuning, administrators can build a comprehensive, high-availability solution that ensures their databases remain accessible and secure, even in the face of failures.

# Database Mirroring and Log Shipping

Database mirroring and log shipping are two key methods used in SQL Server environments to ensure high availability, disaster recovery, and data redundancy. Both techniques are aimed at minimizing downtime and ensuring data consistency by replicating databases across multiple servers. While these solutions offer robust protection against server failures, they come with distinct differences in how they operate, their configuration requirements, and their suitability for different scenarios. Understanding the mechanics of database mirroring and log shipping, as well as when and how to implement them, is essential for database administrators looking to enhance the availability and reliability of their SQL Server infrastructure.

Database mirroring is a high availability solution that maintains two copies of a database on separate SQL Server instances: one as the principal database and the other as the mirrored database. The principal server is where all read and write operations occur, while the mirrored server contains an exact replica of the database. The primary goal of database mirroring is to provide automatic failover capabilities in the event of a failure on the principal server. There are two types of database mirroring configurations: high-safety mode and high-performance mode.

In high-safety mode, database mirroring operates in synchronous mode. This means that every transaction committed to the principal database is simultaneously committed to the mirrored database, ensuring that both databases are in sync at all times. If the principal server fails, the mirrored server can quickly take over, becoming the new principal, with minimal data loss and downtime. The major advantage of high-safety mode is its strong data consistency and reliability, as it ensures that no committed transactions are lost during a failover. However, because transactions must be written to both the principal and mirrored databases simultaneously, there may be a slight performance overhead due to the additional I/O operations.

High-performance mode, in contrast, operates asynchronously. In this mode, transactions on the principal server are committed to the mirrored server without waiting for acknowledgment, which allows for faster performance and lower latency. However, the drawback of high-performance mode is that there is a risk of data loss if a failover occurs before the mirrored database has received the latest transactions. This mode is typically used in scenarios where performance is a higher priority than guaranteeing data consistency, such as in environments with geographically distributed servers where network latency would make synchronous replication impractical.

One of the key features of database mirroring is automatic failover. If the principal server becomes unavailable, the mirrored database can be automatically promoted to the principal role, ensuring that database services remain operational. Automatic failover is available only when the configuration includes a witness server, which helps to monitor the health of the principal and mirrored servers. The witness server ensures that the system can determine the health of both servers and automatically initiate failover without requiring manual intervention. Database mirroring also provides a quick recovery mechanism, allowing the mirrored server to quickly take over with little impact on users.

However, SQL Server database mirroring is a feature that has limitations. It is only applicable to a single database and does not support the replication of multiple databases within a single configuration. Furthermore, database mirroring is not available in all editions of SQL Server; it is only supported in the Standard and Enterprise editions. Moreover, database mirroring has been superseded by the more comprehensive AlwaysOn Availability Groups feature in recent versions of SQL Server, which provides support for multiple databases and enhanced failover capabilities.

Log shipping, on the other hand, is another high availability and disaster recovery solution that involves periodically backing up the transaction logs of a primary database, copying those log backups to a secondary server, and restoring them to a copy of the database. Unlike database mirroring, log shipping does not provide real-time synchronization of the primary and secondary databases. Instead, it is based on a backup-restore process that occurs at scheduled intervals, typically every 10 to 15 minutes. This makes log shipping a more cost-effective solution for organizations that do not require the same level of real-time synchronization as database mirroring.

Log shipping is implemented by creating a primary server (the primary database) and one or more secondary servers (the secondary databases). The transaction logs are regularly backed up on the primary database, then copied over to the secondary server. On the secondary server, these transaction logs are restored to a copy of the database. In the event of a failure on the primary server, administrators can bring the secondary server online by restoring the latest transaction log backup, ensuring that the database can be recovered to the most recent point in time. This failover process, however, is not automatic and typically requires manual intervention to perform the failover and bring the secondary database online.

One of the advantages of log shipping is that it is relatively simple to configure and does not require the same level of infrastructure as database mirroring. It is supported on all editions of SQL Server, making it a viable solution for smaller organizations or environments that cannot justify the cost of the more advanced AlwaysOn Availability Groups or database mirroring features. Log shipping also allows for multiple secondary databases, which provides flexibility for organizations that require redundancy across multiple locations. Additionally, because log shipping only copies transaction logs rather than replicating entire databases in real time, it has a lower impact on network bandwidth and storage resources.

However, log shipping has its drawbacks. The most significant limitation is the potential for data loss, as there is a delay between when the transaction log is backed up on the primary server and when it is restored on the secondary server. This means that if the primary server fails before the latest transaction log has been copied and restored, data may be lost. Moreover, log shipping does not provide automatic failover, and administrators must manually promote a secondary server to take over the role of the primary server in case of a failure. The manual nature of failover, along with the delay in log shipping, makes it less suitable for high-availability environments that require minimal downtime.

Both database mirroring and log shipping offer distinct advantages and limitations, making them suitable for different types of environments. Database mirroring is ideal for applications that require real-time synchronization and automatic failover, providing a high level of data consistency with minimal downtime. However, it is limited to single databases and does not support the replication of multiple databases or large-scale environments. Log shipping, on the other hand, is more flexible and cost-effective, allowing for the protection of multiple databases and the use of less expensive infrastructure. However, its lack of real-time synchronization and automatic failover means that it may not be appropriate for organizations that require continuous availability and immediate failover capabilities.

Both solutions can play an important role in a comprehensive high availability and disaster recovery strategy. By understanding their strengths and limitations, administrators can choose the appropriate solution based on their organization's needs, ensuring that data remains protected and available even in the face of hardware failures or other disasters. Whether using database mirroring for real-time failover or log shipping for periodic synchronization, these features are essential for maintaining a resilient and reliable SQL Server environment.

# SQL Server Replication and Synchronization

SQL Server replication and synchronization are essential features for distributing data across multiple locations, ensuring that data is consistent, and enabling applications to operate efficiently across different environments. Replication is a process where data from one server, known as the publisher, is copied to one or more other servers, called subscribers. This can be done in various configurations, allowing for a flexible approach to data distribution and ensuring that the data is available in multiple places without compromising performance or availability. Synchronization, on the other hand, involves ensuring that the data in these replicated databases remains consistent across all locations, even as updates or changes occur. SQL Server provides several types of replication, including snapshot replication, transactional replication, and merge replication, each with unique characteristics suited to different business needs. Understanding how these methods work, their benefits, and their limitations is crucial for database administrators to effectively implement replication and synchronization solutions.

Snapshot replication is one of the simplest forms of replication in SQL Server. It involves taking a snapshot of a database at a given point in time and copying the entire contents of the database or selected tables to a subscriber. The snapshot is applied in its entirety to the subscriber, meaning that it replaces the existing data at the subscriber with the data from the snapshot. This type of replication is ideal for situations where the data does not change frequently, or where it is acceptable for the data at the subscriber to be periodically replaced with the latest copy from the publisher. Snapshot replication is particularly useful when there is a need to replicate large datasets in situations where the overhead of keeping data continuously synchronized is not a concern. However, the downside of snapshot replication is that it can result in higher resource consumption, especially when the entire dataset needs to be copied over each time, which may cause performance issues if the data changes frequently.

Transactional replication, on the other hand, is more sophisticated and suitable for scenarios where data is continuously changing. In transactional replication, changes made to the data at the publisher, such as inserts, updates, and deletes, are immediately replicated to the subscriber. This type of replication is more efficient than snapshot replication because it only replicates the changes, rather than the entire dataset. The process of transactional replication is designed to ensure that data changes are replicated in near real-time, which is critical for high-availability systems that require up-to-date data across multiple locations. Transactional replication uses a transaction log to track changes and then applies those changes to the subscriber as they occur. This method ensures that the replicated data at the subscriber remains consistent with the publisher, making it suitable for systems that require precise and real-time synchronization, such as e-commerce platforms or inventory systems.

However, transactional replication does come with certain complexities. Because the changes are propagated in near real-time, it can introduce latency if the system is under heavy load, especially if the network between the publisher and subscriber is slow. Additionally, transactional replication is more resource-intensive than snapshot replication, as it requires continuous monitoring of the transaction logs and the application of changes at the subscriber. Ensuring that the subscriber's database is always synchronized with the publisher's can also require additional management, particularly in large-scale environments with multiple subscribers. Administrators must be diligent in monitoring the system to ensure that replication is not delayed, which could lead to inconsistencies between the publisher and subscriber databases.

Merge replication is another type of replication that is designed for environments where data can be updated at both the publisher and subscriber. Unlike transactional replication, which ensures that updates made to the publisher are reflected at the subscriber, merge replication allows changes to be made at both locations and then synchronizes those changes. This type of replication is commonly used in scenarios where both central and remote locations need to make updates to the same set of data, such as in mobile applications or field-based systems. Merge replication resolves conflicts that arise when changes are made to the same data at both the publisher and subscriber by using conflict resolution policies. The ability to handle data changes at both ends makes merge replication more flexible, but it also introduces a higher level of complexity and overhead. Conflict resolution can be configured to automatically resolve conflicts, or administrators can be alerted to conflicts and manually resolve them.

While replication is essential for data distribution and high availability, maintaining synchronization across multiple servers and ensuring that data is consistent can be challenging. Synchronization in SQL Server replication ensures that the data at the publisher and subscriber are consistent, even if changes are made on both ends. The synchronization process relies heavily on the type of replication being used. In transactional and merge replication, SQL Server provides the capability to detect and resolve conflicts, ensuring that data integrity is maintained. For example, in merge replication, if the same record is updated on both the publisher and subscriber, the system must determine which update takes precedence. Conflict resolution is an integral part of this process and can be customized to meet the needs of the application, either through automatic conflict resolution rules or manual intervention.

Additionally, the network and infrastructure used for replication play a significant role in ensuring synchronization. Replication requires a stable and reliable network connection between the publisher and subscriber, as any interruptions can result in delays in applying changes. In environments where the network may experience downtime or instability, administrators need to configure replication agents that can handle network failures and ensure that replication resumes once connectivity is restored. SQL Server offers several types of replication agents, such as the Distribution Agent and Merge Agent, that help to monitor and manage replication and synchronization tasks. These agents play a crucial role in ensuring that the changes made on the publisher are correctly applied to the subscribers, keeping the data synchronized across all locations.

Replication in SQL Server can also be leveraged for other purposes, such as offloading reporting workloads from the primary database. By using replication to distribute read-only copies of data to secondary servers, organizations can ensure that reporting and analytics do not place undue strain on the primary transactional database. This is particularly useful in high-traffic environments where reporting queries could affect the performance of transactional systems. By replicating the data to separate servers dedicated to reporting, businesses can improve performance, ensure high availability, and provide real-time access to data for analysis and reporting purposes.

In environments with high availability requirements, SQL Server replication and synchronization are indispensable tools for maintaining data consistency across multiple locations. By selecting the appropriate replication method—whether snapshot, transactional, or merge replication—database administrators can ensure that data is properly distributed, synchronized, and available across a variety of servers. Although replication can be complex to set up and manage, the benefits of improved data availability, redundancy, and offloading workloads make it a critical component of a resilient SQL Server infrastructure. Effective management and monitoring of replication systems are key to ensuring that data remains consistent, performance is optimized, and potential issues are addressed promptly, ensuring that the business can continue to operate smoothly and securely.

# Monitoring SQL Server Performance

Monitoring SQL Server performance is an essential task for database administrators who aim to ensure that their systems are running efficiently and reliably. SQL Server is a powerful relational database management system that serves as the backbone for many business-critical applications, and its performance directly impacts the responsiveness and availability of these applications. However, like any complex system, SQL Server is susceptible to performance bottlenecks and other issues that can degrade its efficiency over time. Monitoring performance allows administrators to identify these issues proactively, diagnose the root causes, and implement corrective measures to optimize the server's performance. In this chapter, we will explore the key concepts, tools, and strategies involved in monitoring SQL Server performance, helping administrators ensure that their SQL Server instances run smoothly and efficiently.

The first step in monitoring SQL Server performance is understanding what constitutes good performance. In a typical SQL Server environment, performance can be evaluated across several dimensions, including query execution speed, server resource utilization (such as CPU, memory, and disk I/O), and overall system responsiveness. For instance, long-running queries that consume excessive resources can be a sign of inefficient indexing, poor query design, or inadequate hardware resources. Similarly, high CPU usage, excessive disk activity, or memory bottlenecks can indicate that the server is under stress and may require configuration changes or hardware upgrades. By regularly monitoring these key performance indicators (KPIs), administrators can stay ahead of potential issues before they impact end users.

One of the primary tools for monitoring SQL Server performance is SQL Server Management Studio (SSMS), which provides a comprehensive interface for managing and monitoring SQL Server instances. SSMS includes built-in reports and performance dashboards that offer a high-level overview of server health, resource utilization, and other important metrics. These reports include information on query performance, index usage, disk space, memory consumption, and more. The SSMS interface allows administrators to quickly identify areas of concern and drill down into specific metrics for more detailed analysis.

SQL Server also provides a powerful tool called SQL Server Profiler, which allows administrators to capture and analyze events and queries that are being executed on the server in real time. SQL Server Profiler provides deep insights into query performance by capturing detailed data about each query, including execution times, resource usage, and any errors that may have occurred during execution. Administrators can use Profiler to identify slow-running queries, find bottlenecks in query execution, and monitor the behavior of individual SQL statements. By analyzing Profiler data, administrators can make informed decisions about query optimization, indexing strategies, and other performance-related improvements.

Another critical tool for monitoring SQL Server performance is Dynamic Management Views (DMVs). DMVs are a set of system views that provide real-time information about the internal workings of SQL Server. These views expose a wealth of information about server health, query performance, and system resources. DMVs can be queried to retrieve detailed data about CPU usage, memory allocation, disk I/O, locking, blocking, and query execution plans. By regularly querying DMVs, administrators can gain deep insights into how SQL Server is performing and identify any areas where resources are being overused or underutilized. Commonly used DMVs include sys.dm_exec_requests, which provides information about currently executing queries, and sys.dm_exec_query_stats, which shows statistics about query execution performance.

In addition to SSMS, SQL Server Profiler, and DMVs, SQL Server includes the Windows Performance Monitor (PerfMon), a built-in tool that tracks system-level performance metrics such as CPU usage, disk I/O, memory usage, and network activity. PerfMon can be used in conjunction with SQL Server's native monitoring tools to provide a more comprehensive view of server performance. By tracking hardware-level performance alongside SQL Server-specific metrics, administrators can get a clearer picture of where performance issues may be occurring. For example, if CPU usage is high and SQL Server queries are running slowly, administrators may need to investigate both SQL Server query optimization and the overall CPU performance on the host machine.

SQL Server also offers Resource Governor, a tool that allows administrators to manage SQL Server resource usage by controlling CPU and memory allocation for different workloads. Resource Governor allows SQL Server to prioritize certain queries or workloads, ensuring that critical tasks receive the resources they need while limiting the impact of less important tasks. By using Resource Governor, administrators can prevent resource contention and ensure that SQL Server performs optimally even during periods of heavy load.

Disk I/O is one of the most common performance bottlenecks in SQL Server environments. SQL Server relies heavily on disk subsystems to store and retrieve data, so disk I/O performance can significantly affect query performance. Administrators should regularly monitor disk I/O performance using DMVs and PerfMon, paying particular attention to disk queue lengths and read/write latency. High disk latency or long queue lengths may indicate that the disk subsystem is underperforming and may need to be upgraded or optimized. Administrators can also use the SQL Server Disk Usage report in SSMS to monitor disk space usage and identify tables or indexes that may be consuming excessive storage.

Memory management is another critical area for SQL Server performance. SQL Server uses memory to cache data and execution plans, which helps to improve query performance by reducing disk I/O. However, if SQL Server is allocated too much memory or if the system does not have enough memory to handle the workload, performance can suffer. To monitor memory usage, administrators can use DMVs like sys.dm_os_memory_clerks, which provides information about SQL Server's memory allocation, and sys.dm_exec_query_memory_grants, which shows memory usage for specific queries. Administrators should also ensure that the SQL Server instance is configured with the appropriate maximum memory settings to prevent SQL Server from consuming all available system memory and starving other applications.

One of the most common performance issues in SQL Server is inefficient query execution. Poorly written queries can cause excessive CPU usage, high disk I/O, and long response times. To diagnose query performance issues, administrators can use execution plans, which provide a detailed breakdown of how SQL Server executes a query.

Execution plans show the steps SQL Server takes to process a query, including table scans, index seeks, joins, and other operations. By analyzing execution plans, administrators can identify inefficient operations and suggest optimizations, such as creating indexes, rewriting queries, or adjusting SQL Server configuration settings. Tools like Query Store, which tracks the history of query execution plans and performance metrics, can also help administrators monitor long-term query performance trends and identify queries that may need optimization.

Regular performance tuning is essential for maintaining optimal SQL Server performance over time. As workloads change, indexes become fragmented, and data grows, administrators must continue to monitor and adjust SQL Server configurations and queries. Tasks like rebuilding indexes, updating statistics, and optimizing queries should be performed on a regular basis to ensure that SQL Server continues to run efficiently. Additionally, administrators should consider setting up automated alerts for key performance metrics, such as CPU usage, disk space, or query execution time, to ensure that any performance degradation is detected and addressed promptly.

SQL Server performance monitoring is an ongoing process that involves using a combination of built-in tools, such as SSMS, SQL Server Profiler, DMVs, PerfMon, and Resource Governor, to track server health, resource utilization, and query performance. By continuously monitoring these metrics and optimizing SQL Server configurations and queries, administrators can ensure that the database environment operates efficiently and reliably. Effective performance monitoring helps to prevent issues before they become critical, ensuring that users and applications experience minimal disruption and that the SQL Server instance remains a high-performing, resilient component of the IT infrastructure.

# Identifying and Resolving Performance Bottlenecks

SQL Server is a complex and powerful relational database management system, and like any sophisticated software, it can experience performance bottlenecks. These bottlenecks can manifest as slow query execution, high resource usage, or degraded system responsiveness, all of which can impact the user experience and disrupt business operations. Identifying and resolving performance bottlenecks is a crucial part of SQL Server administration, as it ensures that the database environment runs smoothly, efficiently, and reliably. Addressing performance issues requires a deep understanding of how SQL Server works, the various factors that influence its performance, and the tools available to diagnose and resolve these issues. This chapter will explore the process of identifying and resolving SQL Server performance bottlenecks, focusing on common sources of performance degradation and the best practices for addressing them.

The first step in identifying performance bottlenecks is understanding the key metrics that affect SQL Server performance. CPU utilization, memory usage, disk I/O, and network activity are the primary resources that SQL Server consumes, and any of these can become a bottleneck if they are overutilized or misconfigured. High CPU usage is often the result of inefficient queries, lack of proper indexing, or excessive background processes. Memory issues, such as insufficient memory allocation or memory leaks, can lead to slow query performance, especially in systems with large datasets. Disk I/O bottlenecks are common in systems that require frequent data reads and writes, as SQL Server depends heavily on the disk subsystem to store and retrieve data. Network issues can also contribute to bottlenecks, especially in environments where SQL Server replicas or remote connections are used.

Once the critical resources have been identified, the next step is to monitor their usage in real time to detect potential bottlenecks. SQL Server provides several tools for monitoring system performance, including SQL Server Management Studio (SSMS), SQL Server Profiler, Dynamic Management Views (DMVs), and Windows Performance Monitor. These tools allow administrators to track resource usage and identify performance issues. For instance, SQL Server Profiler captures real-time query activity and can help identify long-running or resource-intensive queries. DMVs, such as sys.dm_exec_requests and sys.dm_exec_query_stats, provide detailed information about current query execution, resource consumption, and blocking. By analyzing these metrics, administrators can pinpoint which queries or operations are consuming excessive resources and focus their optimization efforts on those areas.

One of the most common performance bottlenecks in SQL Server is poor query performance. Inefficient queries can cause excessive CPU usage, memory consumption, and disk I/O, leading to slow system performance. Identifying slow-running queries is crucial to resolving bottlenecks. Administrators can use execution plans to analyze how SQL Server processes queries and where performance issues arise. Execution plans show the sequence of operations that SQL Server performs to execute a query, including table scans, index seeks, joins, and sorting operations. By analyzing the execution plan, administrators can identify costly operations that contribute to performance degradation. For example, a table scan can be significantly slower than an index seek, so administrators may need to create or optimize indexes to speed up query execution.

Another common source of performance bottlenecks is missing or inefficient indexes. Indexes are essential for speeding up data retrieval, but if they are poorly designed or outdated, they can cause SQL Server to perform unnecessary full table scans, resulting in slow query performance. Administrators should regularly review and optimize indexes, ensuring that they cover the most frequently queried columns. Index fragmentation is another issue that can affect performance, especially on large tables with frequent insert, update, or delete operations. Rebuilding or reorganizing fragmented indexes can help improve performance by reducing the overhead of maintaining inefficient index structures. Additionally, administrators should avoid over-indexing, as having too many indexes can slow down write operations, such as inserts and updates, due to the need to maintain the indexes.

Another significant contributor to performance bottlenecks is blocking, which occurs when one query holds a lock on a resource that prevents other queries from accessing it. Blocking can result in poor system performance and slow query execution, particularly in high-concurrency environments. SQL Server uses locks to maintain data consistency, but excessive locking can cause delays. To identify blocking issues, administrators can use DMVs like sys.dm_exec_requests and sys.dm_exec_sessions, which provide information about queries that are currently being blocked and the sessions causing the blocking. Once blocking is identified, administrators can take steps to resolve it by optimizing queries to reduce lock contention, using appropriate isolation levels, or implementing techniques like row-level locking or optimistic concurrency control to minimize the impact of locks.

Memory-related bottlenecks are also common in SQL Server, particularly in systems that handle large datasets or complex queries. SQL Server uses memory to cache data, execution plans, and other resources, so inadequate memory can lead to poor performance. When SQL Server runs out of memory, it may have to swap data to disk, resulting in significant performance degradation. Administrators should monitor memory usage using DMVs like sys.dm_os_memory_clerks and sys.dm_exec_query_memory_grants, which provide information about memory consumption by SQL Server and individual queries. If SQL Server is consuming too much memory, administrators may need to adjust the maximum memory setting for the instance, optimize queries to reduce memory usage, or add more physical memory to the server. Memory pressure can also occur when SQL Server is competing with other applications for system resources, so it is essential to ensure that SQL Server is allocated enough memory for optimal performance.

Disk I/O bottlenecks are another common issue that can degrade SQL Server performance. SQL Server relies heavily on disk subsystems to store and retrieve data, and if the disk system is not optimized or has insufficient throughput, performance can suffer. High disk latency, long queue lengths, or insufficient disk space can all contribute to performance bottlenecks. Administrators should monitor disk performance using tools like Windows Performance Monitor and DMVs such as sys.dm_io_virtual_file_stats, which provide real-time information about disk read and write operations. To alleviate disk I/O bottlenecks, administrators can optimize storage by placing data files, log files, and tempdb on separate physical disks or using faster storage systems, such as solid-state drives (SSDs). Additionally, ensuring that the disk subsystem has enough capacity to handle the workload is essential for maintaining SQL Server performance.

In environments with high concurrency or large datasets, SQL Server performance can be affected by issues such as deadlocks, which occur when two or more queries are unable to complete because they are each waiting for resources held by the other. Deadlocks can cause queries to fail, disrupt operations, and impact system performance. SQL Server provides tools for detecting and resolving deadlocks, such as the deadlock graph, which shows the sequence of events leading to a deadlock. Administrators can use the deadlock graph to identify the queries involved and take steps to resolve the issue, such as optimizing queries to reduce lock contention or modifying the database schema to eliminate circular dependencies.

SQL Server performance bottlenecks can also arise from misconfigured system settings. For example, inadequate configuration of tempdb, SQL Server's system database used for temporary storage of data, can lead to slow performance, particularly in environments with high transaction volumes or large amounts of temporary data. Optimizing tempdb by placing it on fast storage, configuring multiple data files, and ensuring it is sized appropriately for the workload can help alleviate performance issues. Similarly, improper configuration of SQL Server's I/O settings, such as setting up appropriate filegroups and ensuring that data and log files are placed on separate physical disks, can reduce I/O contention and improve performance.

Addressing SQL Server performance bottlenecks requires a combination of monitoring, diagnosis, and optimization. Administrators need to continually monitor system resources, analyze query performance, identify and resolve blocking and locking issues, optimize memory and disk usage, and ensure that the SQL Server instance is configured correctly. By proactively identifying performance issues and applying best practices for query optimization, indexing, memory management, and disk configuration, database administrators can ensure that SQL Server operates at peak efficiency and provides a high level of performance for users and applications.

# Advanced Query Optimization Techniques

Query optimization is a critical aspect of SQL Server performance, especially in environments with large datasets and complex applications. While basic query optimization techniques, such as proper indexing and query rewriting, can go a long way in improving performance, advanced optimization techniques provide deeper insights and more fine-grained control over how SQL Server processes queries. These advanced techniques focus on improving query execution plans, optimizing resource usage, reducing bottlenecks, and ensuring that queries perform as efficiently as possible. This chapter will explore some of the advanced query optimization techniques available in SQL Server, focusing on execution plan analysis, query refactoring, indexing strategies, and optimizing specific SQL constructs.

One of the most powerful tools for advanced query optimization is the query execution plan. The execution plan is SQL Server's roadmap for how it will execute a given query, and analyzing this plan is essential for identifying performance bottlenecks and inefficiencies. The execution plan details every step SQL Server takes to retrieve data, including table scans, index seeks, joins, and sorts. It also provides information about the resources used for each operation, such as CPU, memory, and disk I/O. By examining the execution plan, administrators can identify costly operations that consume excessive resources and make adjustments to improve performance.

One common optimization technique involves identifying and addressing table scans, which are often one of the most expensive operations in a query. A table scan occurs when SQL Server has to read through every row in a table to find the requested data. This is particularly inefficient for large tables, as it results in high disk I/O and slow query execution times. Table scans can often be avoided by creating appropriate indexes on the columns used in the WHERE clause, JOIN conditions, or ORDER BY clauses. By ensuring that queries can utilize indexes efficiently, administrators can significantly reduce the number of rows that SQL Server needs to read, resulting in faster query performance.

Another critical area for optimization is the join strategy used in queries. Joins are common in complex SQL queries and can become a source of performance issues if not handled properly. The most common join types in SQL Server are nested loops, hash joins, and merge joins, each of which has its own performance characteristics. Nested loop joins are typically efficient when joining small datasets or when the outer table is small and the inner table is indexed. However, they can be inefficient for large tables with no appropriate indexes. Hash joins are often used when SQL Server cannot find an index to perform the join, but they can be resource-intensive, particularly when working with large datasets. Merge joins are efficient for sorted datasets, but they require that both tables be sorted on the join column, which can introduce additional overhead.

To optimize joins, it is essential to understand the data distribution and the indexing strategies in place. In cases where SQL Server chooses a suboptimal join strategy, administrators can rewrite the query to provide hints, forcing SQL Server to use a specific join method. For example, using the OPTION (LOOP JOIN) hint forces SQL Server to use a nested loop join, even if it might choose a different strategy. However, using query hints should be done with caution, as they can sometimes override the optimizer's ability to make the best decision based on the data.

Another advanced optimization technique is optimizing subqueries, which are often a source of performance problems. Subqueries can sometimes result in inefficient query plans, especially when they are used in WHERE clauses or SELECT lists. One approach to optimizing subqueries is to rewrite them as joins, as joins are typically more efficient than subqueries, especially in cases where the subquery returns a large result set. In some cases, converting a correlated subquery into a derived table or a common table expression (CTE) can also improve performance, as it allows SQL Server to handle the subquery's results more efficiently.

CTEs themselves are another tool for query optimization. They provide a way to simplify complex queries and can help SQL Server optimize the query execution plan. However, CTEs can also introduce performance issues if not used carefully, particularly if they are recursive or involve large result sets. In some cases, administrators can improve performance by converting a CTE into a temporary table or table variable, especially if the CTE is used multiple times in the query. This allows SQL Server to materialize the intermediate results and avoid re-executing the CTE's logic multiple times.

Index optimization is another key element of advanced query optimization. While creating the right indexes is essential for query performance, maintaining and optimizing those indexes is just as important. Over time, indexes can become fragmented, which increases the time it takes for SQL Server to find and retrieve data. Fragmented indexes result in inefficient reads from disk, as SQL Server must read more pages than necessary to access the indexed data. Regular index maintenance, such as rebuilding or reorganizing fragmented indexes, can help restore performance by ensuring that indexes remain efficient. Administrators can use the sys.dm_db_index_physical_stats DMV to monitor index fragmentation levels and determine when maintenance is needed.

However, creating too many indexes can also degrade performance, especially for write-heavy systems. Each time a record is inserted, updated, or deleted, SQL Server must update all relevant indexes. This can lead to increased disk I/O and slower write operations. Therefore, it's crucial to strike a balance between having enough indexes to improve query performance and avoiding unnecessary indexes that add overhead to data modification operations. Indexing strategies should be carefully reviewed to ensure that only the most critical columns are indexed, based on query patterns and data access needs.

SQL Server also provides the ability to use filtered indexes, which allow administrators to create indexes that cover only a subset of data. This can be particularly useful for large tables with columns that have a small number of distinct values. By creating a filtered index that only covers rows with specific values, administrators can reduce the size of the index and improve query performance by narrowing the scope of the index.

Another optimization technique involves optimizing the use of functions and expressions in queries. While SQL Server provides powerful functions for manipulating data, such as string, date, and mathematical functions, these functions can sometimes slow down query performance, especially when used in WHERE clauses or JOIN conditions. For example, using a function on a column in a WHERE clause can prevent SQL Server from using an index, forcing it to scan the entire table. To optimize queries that involve functions, administrators can consider precomputing values in the application or storing computed columns in the database, which allows SQL Server to use indexes efficiently.

Finally, optimizing concurrency and reducing locking contention is crucial for high-performance systems, particularly in environments with high transaction volumes. SQL Server provides several isolation levels that determine how transactions interact with each other and how locks are acquired. While higher isolation levels, such as Serializable, provide stronger consistency, they can also increase blocking and deadlock occurrences, which can degrade performance. By carefully choosing the appropriate isolation level for each workload, administrators can reduce locking contention and improve query throughput.

Advanced query optimization techniques in SQL Server are essential for achieving high performance, especially in large-scale and complex environments. By analyzing execution plans, optimizing indexes, refactoring queries, and carefully managing concurrency and resource utilization, administrators can ensure that SQL Server queries run efficiently and deliver optimal performance. Regular monitoring, combined with a solid understanding of SQL Server's query execution mechanics, allows administrators to proactively identify and resolve performance bottlenecks, ensuring that the system remains responsive and capable of handling increasing workloads.

# Managing SQL Server TempDB for Performance

TempDB is a crucial system database in SQL Server, used for storing temporary objects such as temporary tables, stored procedures, worktables, and intermediate results for query processing. Despite being a system database, TempDB plays a significant role in the overall performance of SQL Server, and its configuration and management can have a direct impact on the performance of queries and operations. Given its importance, ensuring that TempDB is optimized for performance is essential for maintaining SQL Server's efficiency and responsiveness. This chapter will delve into best practices and strategies for managing SQL Server TempDB, focusing on configuration, resource allocation, and maintenance, with the goal of maximizing performance and minimizing bottlenecks.

TempDB is used by SQL Server to store temporary objects for all active sessions. This means that every query, whether it is complex or simple, may interact with TempDB, making it a shared resource for all users and applications. As a result, TempDB can quickly become a performance bottleneck if not managed correctly. When TempDB runs into performance issues, it can result in poor query execution, slow response times, and high contention for resources. Therefore, understanding how TempDB operates and taking proactive steps to configure and optimize it is crucial for SQL Server performance.

One of the first steps in optimizing TempDB is ensuring that it is properly sized. By default, TempDB is created with a small initial size and limited space, which may not be sufficient for handling larger workloads or complex queries. If TempDB is too small, SQL Server may need to allocate additional space dynamically, which can lead to disk fragmentation and delays as space is allocated. To prevent this, administrators should pre-allocate enough space to TempDB to avoid frequent autogrowth events. Autogrowth can be a significant performance issue because it requires SQL Server to stop processing queries temporarily while it allocates additional space. By setting appropriate initial sizes based on the expected workload, administrators can ensure that TempDB has enough room to operate efficiently.

TempDB is a shared resource used by all sessions in SQL Server, so managing its I/O operations is vital for preventing performance degradation. Disk contention can occur when multiple queries simultaneously access TempDB, leading to high I/O demands and potential slowdowns. To alleviate this, it is recommended to place TempDB on dedicated, high-performance storage. Ideally, TempDB should be located on fast disks, such as Solid-State Drives (SSDs), to minimize I/O latency. Additionally, it is important to ensure that TempDB is located on separate storage from other critical SQL Server files, such as data files and log files. This separation helps distribute I/O operations and reduces contention, ensuring that TempDB has the resources it needs to perform optimally without affecting other databases.

Another key aspect of TempDB management is ensuring that it has sufficient data files to handle concurrent workloads efficiently. In SQL Server, TempDB uses a single data file by default. However, in systems with high concurrency, a single TempDB data file can become a bottleneck, as SQL Server uses a proportional fill algorithm to allocate space in the data files. This means that if there is only one data file, all queries and processes accessing TempDB will contend for the same file, leading to performance issues. The solution to this is to add multiple data files to TempDB, which allows SQL Server to distribute the workload across the files and reduces contention. The number of data files should generally be equal to the number of CPU cores on the system, up to eight files. Beyond eight files, the benefits of adding more data files begin to diminish, and administrators should focus on other optimization techniques.

Once the number of data files is configured, administrators should monitor the space usage across all TempDB data files to ensure that the files are being used efficiently. If one data file is consistently filling up faster than the others, it could indicate a problem with the proportional fill algorithm or that certain queries are disproportionately accessing a specific data file. In such cases, administrators can consider adjusting the file allocation to optimize performance further. Regular monitoring of TempDB's space usage is essential to ensure that no data file becomes full, as this would cause SQL Server to stop processing queries, resulting in a severe performance issue.

In addition to data files, TempDB's transaction log file is another area that requires attention for performance optimization. Like other SQL Server databases, TempDB uses a transaction log to record modifications to the database. However, because TempDB is used for temporary storage, its transaction log can grow rapidly, particularly during large queries or operations involving large sorts, joins, or aggregates. To prevent the transaction log from becoming a bottleneck, administrators should ensure that it is located on high-performance storage, just like the TempDB data files. Moreover, it is important to monitor the size of the TempDB transaction log and configure it appropriately to prevent it from growing uncontrollably. Regularly backing up the transaction log can also help ensure that it does not become too large and negatively impact performance.

Another factor that can impact TempDB performance is the configuration of SQL Server's MaxDOP (Maximum Degree of Parallelism) setting. When MaxDOP is set to a high value, SQL Server may attempt to parallelize queries across multiple CPU cores, which can result in increased contention for TempDB resources. In some cases, this can lead to performance degradation, as multiple threads may compete for access to the same TempDB data files. To mitigate this issue, administrators can adjust the MaxDOP setting to a lower value to limit the number of threads that can simultaneously access TempDB, reducing contention and improving overall performance.

TempDB performance can also be impacted by certain SQL Server features and workloads. For example, complex queries that involve large sorts, hash joins, or aggregations often require TempDB to store intermediate results, which can lead to excessive disk usage and I/O contention. In these cases, administrators should review query execution plans and optimize the queries to minimize the use of TempDB. In some cases, creating indexes or rewriting queries to reduce the need for temporary storage can help reduce the strain on TempDB.

SQL Server provides several system views and dynamic management views (DMVs) that allow administrators to monitor TempDB usage and diagnose performance issues. For example, the sys.dm_db_file_space_usage DMV provides information on the space used by each TempDB data file, while sys.dm_exec_requests shows queries currently executing that may be using TempDB heavily. By regularly querying these DMVs, administrators can track TempDB usage, identify queries that are consuming excessive resources, and take appropriate action to optimize performance.

Proper maintenance and regular monitoring of TempDB are essential to ensuring that SQL Server operates efficiently and without bottlenecks. Administrators should configure TempDB based on the server's workload, optimize disk usage, and regularly monitor resource consumption. By applying best practices for TempDB management, such as ensuring sufficient data files, monitoring disk I/O, and managing the transaction log, administrators can minimize performance issues and ensure that SQL Server runs smoothly. TempDB is a shared resource that is used by all queries, so its performance directly impacts the overall system. Proper configuration, maintenance, and monitoring are key to preventing TempDB from becoming a performance bottleneck and ensuring that SQL Server operates at peak efficiency.

# SQL Server Storage Optimization and Configuration

SQL Server is a highly efficient relational database management system that relies heavily on its underlying storage infrastructure. The performance and scalability of SQL Server are directly affected by how data is stored and accessed, making storage optimization and configuration critical for ensuring that the database operates efficiently. Proper configuration of SQL Server storage can reduce I/O bottlenecks, minimize latency, and ensure that queries execute quickly, even under heavy workloads. Optimizing SQL Server storage involves more than simply allocating disk space; it requires thoughtful consideration of disk placement, file layout, I/O distribution, and monitoring to ensure that the system performs at its best. This chapter explores the key aspects of SQL Server storage optimization and configuration, covering disk subsystem setup, data and log file management, and performance tuning strategies to achieve optimal storage performance.

The foundation of SQL Server storage optimization lies in the proper selection and configuration of the physical disk subsystem. SQL Server's storage architecture relies on efficient data retrieval and storage, making the choice of storage hardware essential for optimal performance. A common best practice for optimizing storage is to separate SQL Server's data files, log files, and TempDB onto different physical disks or storage devices. This distribution of workloads across multiple disks helps prevent I/O contention and ensures that SQL Server has dedicated resources for each type of data operation. By placing the transaction logs on a separate disk from the data files, for instance, SQL Server can handle the high-frequency read/write operations of the logs without impacting the performance of the data files. Similarly, separating TempDB onto its own disk further optimizes disk I/O, as TempDB is heavily used by SQL Server during query execution, especially for complex operations such as sorting or joins.

When configuring disk storage, it is important to consider the performance characteristics of the storage hardware. Using solid-state drives (SSDs) for SQL Server's data files and transaction logs can greatly improve performance, as SSDs have much faster read and write speeds compared to traditional spinning hard disk drives (HDDs). SSDs reduce I/O latency, which is critical for SQL Server, especially in environments with high transaction volumes or large databases. However, for organizations that may not have access to high-performance SSDs, optimizing the configuration of HDDs can still provide good performance, particularly when using RAID configurations that offer redundancy and improved throughput. RAID 10 is commonly recommended for SQL Server's data files due to its balance of redundancy and performance. By combining RAID 1's mirroring with RAID 0's striping, RAID 10 offers fault tolerance along with improved read and write speeds, making it a good choice for critical databases.

Once the physical disk subsystem is properly configured, the next step in storage optimization is managing SQL Server's database and transaction log files. SQL Server stores data in database files with an extension of .mdf for the primary data file and .ndf for secondary data files. These files contain all the data stored in SQL Server's tables, indexes, and other objects. Transaction log files, with an extension of .ldf, are used to track changes to the database and ensure data consistency. Proper management of these files is essential to ensure that SQL Server performs optimally. It is important to configure SQL Server's file system to have an appropriate number of files based on the workload and the number of CPU cores. A common recommendation is to create multiple data files for SQL Server databases to improve disk I/O and reduce contention. As a general guideline, the number of data files should be equal to the number of CPU cores on the server, up to a maximum of eight files. This configuration allows SQL Server to distribute I/O operations across multiple files, reducing the likelihood of I/O bottlenecks that can occur when using a single data file.

When configuring transaction log files, it is crucial to allocate sufficient space to handle the transaction volume of SQL Server. Transaction log files should be sized appropriately to avoid frequent autogrowth events, which can lead to performance degradation. Autogrowth operations can be costly, as they require SQL Server to pause processing while allocating additional space, and they can lead to disk fragmentation. Administrators should set the transaction log file to a fixed size that accounts for the database's transaction processing needs. If the transaction log grows too large, SQL Server may experience delays during log backup operations. Regular transaction log backups should also be scheduled to prevent the log file from growing uncontrollably, as a large transaction log can result in inefficient disk usage and slow down SQL Server.

In addition to file management, SQL Server performance can be further optimized through proper file placement and configuration. Filegroups in SQL Server allow administrators to organize database objects into logical groups, making it easier to distribute data across multiple physical disks. For example, frequently accessed tables or indexes can be placed on separate filegroups, reducing disk contention and improving I/O performance. Filegroups also allow administrators to back up and restore parts of the database independently, providing greater flexibility and performance during backup operations. By using multiple filegroups, SQL Server can optimize disk utilization and improve query performance by placing high-demand objects on high-performance storage devices, while less frequently accessed data can be placed on slower, more cost-effective storage.

In addition to managing physical files, administrators should also configure SQL Server's internal memory and I/O settings to optimize storage performance. SQL Server relies heavily on memory for caching data, query execution plans, and index structures, so ensuring that memory is properly allocated and managed is critical for performance.

SQL Server automatically handles memory allocation, but administrators can set upper limits for the amount of memory SQL Server can use, ensuring that other applications and system processes have enough memory to function. Similarly, SQL Server's I/O settings, such as the number of I/O threads and the max degree of parallelism (MaxDOP), can be adjusted to optimize the way SQL Server interacts with disk subsystems. For example, reducing the number of parallel threads can help avoid overloading the disk subsystem when running complex queries that require heavy I/O operations.

Storage performance is also impacted by the management of TempDB, SQL Server's system database used for temporary storage of intermediate results during query execution. TempDB is heavily used for tasks such as sorting, hashing, and storing intermediate results, making it a critical component of SQL Server performance. To optimize TempDB, administrators should ensure that it is placed on a dedicated disk, separate from the data and log files. TempDB's performance can also be improved by configuring multiple data files for TempDB, similar to the configuration for user databases. By creating a number of data files proportional to the number of CPU cores, SQL Server can reduce contention and improve TempDB's performance under heavy workloads.

Another aspect of SQL Server storage optimization is monitoring and maintaining storage over time. As the database grows and usage patterns change, regular monitoring of disk space, disk I/O performance, and file growth is essential for maintaining optimal performance. SQL Server provides a number of tools for monitoring storage usage, such as the sys.dm_db_file_space_usage dynamic management view, which shows the current usage of each file in the database, and the SQL Server Error Log, which provides details on any storage-related issues. Administrators should also perform regular disk defragmentation and index maintenance tasks to ensure that storage performance remains optimal.

SQL Server storage optimization is an ongoing process that requires attention to detail in both the initial configuration and ongoing maintenance. By properly configuring the disk subsystem, managing database and transaction log files, and utilizing features like filegroups and TempDB optimization, administrators can ensure that SQL Server performs efficiently and can handle growing workloads. Regular monitoring, combined with best practices for disk layout, memory management, and I/O optimization, will help maintain SQL Server's performance, reduce bottlenecks, and ensure that the database environment remains scalable and responsive.

# SQL Server Memory Management and Optimization

Memory management is one of the most critical aspects of SQL Server performance, as it directly impacts query execution, system responsiveness, and resource utilization. SQL Server is a resource-intensive application, and its ability to utilize memory efficiently plays a significant role in ensuring that queries are executed quickly and that the database engine can handle large volumes of data. When memory is not properly managed, SQL Server can experience slow query performance, excessive disk I/O, and system instability. Effective memory management and optimization strategies can help ensure that SQL Server runs efficiently, making the best use of available memory resources and providing optimal performance under varying workloads. This chapter explores SQL Server memory management principles and techniques, focusing on configuration, monitoring, and optimization practices to ensure that memory is utilized efficiently.

At the heart of SQL Server's memory management system is the buffer pool, which is the primary area of memory used for caching data pages and execution plans. The buffer pool holds recently accessed data pages in memory, allowing SQL Server to avoid repeated disk I/O operations, which can significantly slow down performance. By caching frequently accessed data in memory, SQL Server can provide faster query responses, especially for large datasets. The size of the buffer pool is determined by the amount of physical memory available on the system, and SQL Server automatically manages this allocation based on workload demands. However, administrators can configure memory settings to optimize SQL Server's use of memory, ensuring that it is neither starved for resources nor consuming more memory than necessary, which could affect other system processes.

SQL Server uses a dynamic memory management model that adjusts the amount of memory allocated based on system demands. The SQL Server instance automatically adjusts the memory used by the buffer pool, but administrators can set upper and lower memory limits to control how much memory SQL Server is allowed to use. These memory limits are critical for ensuring that SQL Server has sufficient memory to perform optimally while not consuming all available system resources. In environments where SQL Server is running alongside other applications, setting memory limits prevents SQL Server from monopolizing memory, which can cause performance degradation for other processes. The minimum memory setting defines the least amount of memory SQL Server can use, while the maximum memory setting determines the upper limit. Adjusting these settings can ensure that SQL Server operates within the bounds of available system memory without negatively impacting other applications.

Memory pressure occurs when SQL Server is unable to obtain enough memory from the operating system to meet its requirements, and this can significantly affect performance. SQL Server uses the memory it is allocated for caching data and other operations, but when the system is under memory pressure, SQL Server may need to flush data pages from the buffer pool to free up memory, leading to increased disk I/O. This can cause slower query performance and increased response times. To alleviate memory pressure, administrators can monitor SQL Server memory usage using Dynamic Management Views (DMVs), such as sys.dm_os_memory_clerks and sys.dm_exec_requests, which provide insights into memory consumption by various SQL Server components. By identifying areas of high memory usage, administrators can take steps to optimize memory allocation and reduce memory contention.

In addition to managing the buffer pool, SQL Server uses memory for other internal purposes, such as query execution, sorting, and hash joins. These operations can be memory-intensive, especially in queries that involve large datasets or complex operations. When SQL Server cannot allocate sufficient memory for these operations, it may resort to using disk-based temporary storage, which can lead to performance degradation. To mitigate this, administrators can monitor the memory grants for queries using DMVs like sys.dm_exec_query_memory_grants, which shows the amount of memory allocated to each query. If queries are consuming excessive memory, administrators can optimize the queries or adjust the maximum memory configuration to ensure that SQL Server has enough resources to handle large queries efficiently.

Another important aspect of memory optimization is managing SQL Server's use of execution plans. Execution plans are stored in memory and are used to determine the most efficient way to execute a query. While execution plans improve performance by reducing the need to recompile queries, they can also consume a significant amount of memory, especially in environments with a high volume of complex queries. In cases where SQL Server is holding too many execution plans in memory, it can cause memory pressure, slowing down the system. Administrators can monitor the memory used by cached execution plans using DMVs like sys.dm_exec_cached_plans, which provides information on the cached plans and their associated memory usage. If memory usage is excessive, administrators can periodically clear the plan cache to free up memory and improve performance. However, clearing the plan cache should be done with caution, as it can lead to query recompilation and temporary performance degradation.

Managing TempDB, SQL Server's system database used for temporary storage of intermediate results, is also crucial for memory optimization. TempDB relies heavily on memory for operations like sorting, hashing, and storing temporary tables. If TempDB runs out of memory, it may start using disk space, which can result in slow performance. Administrators should ensure that TempDB is configured with sufficient memory and disk resources. Placing TempDB on dedicated, high-performance disks and configuring multiple data files for TempDB, based on the number of CPU cores, can help reduce contention and improve performance. Additionally, managing the memory used by TempDB ensures that SQL Server has enough space to process queries efficiently without relying on disk-based storage.

SQL Server also provides a feature called "memory-optimized tables," which allows for in-memory data storage to improve performance for transactional workloads. Memory-optimized tables are stored entirely in memory and use a special type of storage, which can reduce the need for disk-based I/O and improve query performance. This feature is particularly beneficial for high-throughput applications that require low-latency data access. Memory-optimized tables are part of SQL Server's In-Memory OLTP (Online Transaction Processing) engine, and while they provide significant performance benefits, they also require careful memory management to ensure that SQL Server's memory resources are effectively utilized. Administrators should monitor memory usage by memory-optimized tables and adjust memory allocation settings to avoid excessive memory consumption by these tables.

SQL Server also uses a concept called "buffer cache" to hold frequently accessed data in memory. This cache improves performance by reducing the need for disk I/O operations when queries access the same data repeatedly. However, if the buffer cache becomes too large, it can cause SQL Server to consume more memory than necessary, leading to memory pressure. Administrators should monitor the buffer cache usage and adjust SQL Server's memory settings accordingly to avoid this issue. One common method for optimizing buffer cache usage is to ensure that SQL Server's memory configuration is aligned with the available physical memory, preventing SQL Server from using more memory than the system can handle.

SQL Server memory management is a delicate balance between ensuring that SQL Server has enough memory for optimal performance and preventing it from consuming too much memory, which can affect other system processes. By adjusting memory settings, monitoring memory usage, and implementing best practices for memory optimization, administrators can ensure that SQL Server runs efficiently, even under heavy workloads. Memory optimization requires ongoing monitoring and fine-tuning to adapt to changing workloads and query patterns. By understanding how SQL Server uses memory and how to optimize its configuration, administrators can ensure that the system performs well, minimizes memory contention, and provides fast, reliable service to users and applications.

# Understanding SQL Server Transaction Logs

SQL Server transaction logs are essential components of the database management system, as they play a critical role in maintaining data integrity, supporting recovery processes, and ensuring the durability of transactions. The transaction log records all changes made to the database, including insertions, updates, deletions, and schema modifications. These logs allow SQL Server to recover from system failures, maintain a consistent state of the database, and even replicate changes for high availability and disaster recovery purposes. This chapter delves into the function of SQL Server transaction logs, how they work, and the best practices for managing them to ensure optimal performance and data reliability.

The transaction log is a sequential record that captures every change made to the database, including the before and after values of the data, the transaction that made the change, and the timestamp of when the operation occurred. The primary purpose of the transaction log is to provide a means for SQL Server to recover data in the event of a failure. SQL Server uses the Write-Ahead Logging (WAL) protocol, which ensures that changes are first written to the log before they are applied to the database. This guarantees that even in the case of a system crash or unexpected shutdown, SQL Server can recover to a consistent state by replaying the transaction log from the last committed transaction.

Each SQL Server database has a corresponding transaction log that is typically stored in a file with the .ldf extension. The size of the transaction log file can grow dynamically as changes are made to the database, and SQL Server manages this growth based on the transaction log's autogrowth settings. Because the transaction log contains a sequential history of all database changes, it is crucial for both normal operation and recovery processes. SQL Server utilizes the log for operations like rolling back uncommitted transactions during a failure, or for performing point-in-time recovery to a specific transaction.

The transaction log supports different types of recovery models, each with distinct behaviors regarding how transaction log records are managed and retained. SQL Server offers three primary recovery models: Simple, Full, and Bulk-Logged. The Simple recovery model is the least complex and requires minimal transaction log maintenance. In this model, SQL Server automatically truncates the transaction log after each checkpoint, effectively removing committed transaction records from the log. While this reduces the need for manual intervention, it also means that point-in-time recovery is not possible, as the log is continuously truncated.

The Full recovery model provides the most granular level of logging, enabling point-in-time recovery. In this model, the transaction log is not automatically truncated, and all transaction log records are retained until a transaction log backup is performed. This ensures that every change made to the database is fully logged, allowing administrators to restore the database to any point in time. However, the Full recovery model requires more frequent log backups to manage log file growth and avoid excessive disk space consumption. For large databases, regular transaction log backups are critical to maintaining system performance and preventing the transaction log from growing uncontrollably.

The Bulk-Logged recovery model is a hybrid between the Simple and Full recovery models. It allows for less detailed logging of bulk operations, such as bulk imports or index creation, to reduce the impact on the transaction log. However, like the Full recovery model, the Bulk-Logged recovery model requires transaction log backups and supports point-in-time recovery, but it may log less information during bulk operations. The Bulk-Logged recovery model is particularly useful when performing large data import operations or other bulk operations that do not require the same level of logging as normal transactional changes.

One important concept to understand regarding SQL Server transaction logs is the concept of log truncation. Log truncation is the process by which SQL Server removes committed transaction entries from the transaction log to free up space for new transactions. In the Simple recovery model, this happens automatically after each checkpoint, while in the Full and Bulk-Logged recovery models, log truncation occurs after a transaction log backup is performed. Without proper log truncation, the transaction log can grow exponentially, consuming significant disk space and negatively impacting SQL Server performance. Administrators must ensure that transaction log backups are performed regularly to manage log file growth effectively, especially in Full or Bulk-Logged recovery models.

Another aspect of transaction log management is log backups. In the Full and Bulk-Logged recovery models, log backups are essential for preventing the transaction log from growing too large. Each transaction log backup captures a point-in-time snapshot of the transaction log, allowing SQL Server to truncate the log and free up space for new transactions. These log backups are a crucial part of SQL Server's disaster recovery strategy, as they allow administrators to restore the database to a specific point in time, including after an unexpected failure or corruption. Transaction log backups should be scheduled at regular intervals, depending on the volume of transactions and the criticality of the database.

Log file size management is also a key consideration in transaction log optimization. By default, SQL Server dynamically grows the transaction log file when more space is required. However, excessive autogrowth events can cause performance degradation due to the overhead involved in allocating additional space. Administrators should configure appropriate initial sizes for transaction log files to minimize autogrowth events. They should also consider using fixed-size increments for log growth to avoid excessive fragmentation, which can affect disk I/O performance. Additionally, administrators should monitor transaction log file usage regularly and intervene if the log file is approaching its maximum size to prevent potential issues with log growth.

One common issue that arises with SQL Server transaction logs is log backups that are not taken regularly, which can cause the transaction log to grow uncontrollably. When this happens, SQL Server may be unable to free up space within the log, leading to issues such as out-of-disk-space errors or performance degradation. Administrators can use the sys.dm_db_log_stats DMV to monitor transaction log usage and identify situations where log backups are overdue or where the transaction log is growing abnormally. The transaction log file can also be monitored for space usage through the sys.dm_db_log_space_usage DMV, which provides information about the percentage of space used within the log file.

Another critical aspect of transaction log management is ensuring that the transaction log is stored on high-performance, dedicated storage. Because transaction logs are written sequentially, using high-performance storage such as solid-state drives (SSDs) can significantly improve the performance of write-heavy workloads. Storing the transaction log on a dedicated disk separate from data and TempDB files can help avoid I/O contention and ensure that log write operations are fast and efficient.

In environments with high transaction rates, it may also be beneficial to implement log shipping or AlwaysOn Availability Groups for disaster recovery and high availability. These features leverage transaction log shipping to replicate changes to secondary servers, providing fault tolerance and redundancy in case of a primary server failure. Log shipping and replication rely on the transaction log to propagate changes to remote servers, ensuring data consistency across multiple locations.

Proper management of SQL Server transaction logs is essential for maintaining database integrity, ensuring recoverability, and optimizing performance. By understanding how transaction logs work, configuring appropriate recovery models, scheduling regular log backups, and optimizing log file sizes, administrators can ensure that transaction logs serve their purpose efficiently without causing bottlenecks or consuming excessive disk space. Regular monitoring of log usage, implementing best practices for log file management, and ensuring proper disk performance for log files will enable SQL Server to handle high transaction volumes with minimal impact on system performance.

# Automating SQL Server Administration Tasks

SQL Server administration requires consistent effort to ensure that the database system remains available, secure, and performs optimally. However, many administrative tasks, such as backup management, monitoring, and performance tuning, can be repetitive and time-consuming. Automating these tasks can not only save time but also reduce human error, enhance system reliability, and free up administrators to focus on more strategic tasks. Automation in SQL Server administration is a crucial component of modern database management, as it ensures that routine tasks are executed consistently and efficiently. This chapter explores various methods and techniques for automating SQL Server administration tasks, including using SQL Server Agent, PowerShell scripts, maintenance plans, and third-party tools.

One of the primary tools for automation in SQL Server is SQL Server Agent. SQL Server Agent is a component of SQL Server that allows administrators to automate a wide range of tasks, including running queries, executing backups, and scheduling reports. It is a powerful tool that integrates directly with SQL Server, allowing administrators to define jobs that can run on a specified schedule or in response to specific events. These jobs can include database maintenance tasks, such as index rebuilding, updating statistics, or cleaning up transaction logs, as well as complex administrative tasks like performance monitoring and alerting. SQL Server Agent provides a simple interface for defining, scheduling, and managing jobs, making it a valuable tool for administrators seeking to automate repetitive tasks.

SQL Server Agent jobs are composed of one or more steps, with each step corresponding to a specific action, such as executing a Transact-SQL script or running an operating system command. Each job can be configured to run at a specific time, on a recurring schedule, or when a specific event triggers it. For example, an administrator could create a job that runs a backup every night at midnight, or a job that checks for long-running queries and sends an alert to the administrator. The flexibility of SQL Server Agent makes it an essential tool for automating maintenance tasks and ensuring that critical operations are performed regularly without manual intervention.

In addition to SQL Server Agent, PowerShell provides another powerful method for automating SQL Server tasks. PowerShell is a scripting language and automation framework that is widely used for managing and automating a variety of IT tasks, including database administration. SQL Server has a comprehensive set of PowerShell cmdlets that allow administrators to automate tasks such as creating and managing databases, configuring security settings, and monitoring system performance. PowerShell is particularly useful for more complex automation workflows that may involve interactions between SQL Server and other systems or applications.

Using PowerShell, administrators can create scripts to automate tasks that would otherwise require multiple manual steps. For instance, a PowerShell script could be used to automate the creation of databases, configure filegroups, and set up users with the necessary permissions. PowerShell scripts can also be used for monitoring purposes, such as querying the status of SQL Server instances, checking for database integrity, or generating performance reports. PowerShell's versatility and ability to integrate with other Windows-based tools make it an indispensable automation tool for SQL Server administrators.

SQL Server also provides Maintenance Plans, which are another useful way to automate routine administrative tasks. Maintenance plans allow administrators to define workflows that automate essential tasks like database backups, index optimization, database integrity checks, and report generation. Maintenance plans are created using a visual designer in SQL Server Management Studio (SSMS), where administrators can drag and drop predefined tasks onto a design surface and configure them to run on a scheduled basis. This makes it easy for administrators to set up a set of automated maintenance tasks without needing to write complex scripts or commands.

One of the key benefits of using maintenance plans is that they can be easily configured and executed without requiring advanced knowledge of T-SQL or PowerShell. Maintenance plans can also be configured to send notifications upon completion or failure, ensuring that administrators are kept informed about the status of critical tasks. However, while maintenance plans are a great tool for basic automation, they may not be as flexible or powerful as SQL Server Agent jobs or PowerShell scripts when it comes to more complex or customized automation needs.

In addition to SQL Server Agent, PowerShell, and maintenance plans, administrators can also use third-party tools to automate SQL Server administration tasks. Many third-party solutions offer advanced automation features, such as automated backups, performance monitoring, and alerting, and can provide a more comprehensive automation framework for SQL Server environments. These tools often offer enhanced features like centralized management consoles, integration with other enterprise systems, and advanced reporting capabilities. Third-party automation tools can be particularly useful in large-scale environments where SQL Server instances are spread across multiple servers or locations, as they provide a centralized platform for managing and automating administrative tasks.

Another critical aspect of automating SQL Server administration is alerting and monitoring. Automation can be extended to proactive monitoring, where administrators set up automated alerts based on predefined conditions. SQL Server provides built-in features, such as Data Collector and SQL Server Profiler, to monitor system performance, track long-running queries, and detect unusual activity. By automating alerts, administrators can be immediately notified of issues like performance degradation, disk space running low, or failed backups, allowing them to respond quickly before problems escalate.

SQL Server also allows administrators to use Extended Events, which are a lightweight performance monitoring tool that can be used to track and collect data about specific events and activities within SQL Server. Administrators can create custom events to monitor query performance, deadlocks, and other critical system events. These events can be configured to automatically capture and store data for analysis, enabling administrators to gain valuable insights into system behavior and performance without needing to manually run queries or reports.

One of the main advantages of automating SQL Server tasks is the reduction in human error. Manual intervention can introduce mistakes, such as missed backups, incorrect configurations, or delayed maintenance tasks. By automating routine tasks, administrators can ensure that these tasks are executed consistently and reliably. This is especially important in environments with high transaction volumes or mission-critical applications, where even small delays or inconsistencies in database management can lead to significant downtime or data loss.

Automation also plays a vital role in scalability. As organizations grow and the number of SQL Server instances increases, it becomes increasingly difficult to manually manage all aspects of SQL Server administration. Automation allows administrators to manage multiple instances efficiently by providing a centralized platform for defining, scheduling, and monitoring tasks across all servers. This scalability is particularly important in cloud environments, where SQL Server instances may be distributed across different regions or platforms.

In summary, automating SQL Server administration tasks is an essential practice for modern database management. Tools like SQL Server Agent, PowerShell, maintenance plans, and third-party solutions allow administrators to streamline routine tasks, reduce the risk of human error, and improve system reliability. By automating tasks such as backups, performance monitoring, and alerting, administrators can ensure that SQL Server operates efficiently, freeing up time to focus on more strategic aspects of database management. Automation also provides scalability, allowing organizations to manage their growing SQL Server environments with ease and efficiency.

# SQL Server Agent and Job Management

SQL Server Agent is a crucial component of SQL Server that allows database administrators to automate administrative tasks, schedule jobs, and manage the execution of scripts and processes. It is an essential tool for reducing manual intervention and ensuring that critical database maintenance tasks are performed consistently and on schedule. SQL Server Agent is designed to help administrators streamline operations such as backups, index maintenance, database integrity checks, and reporting, all of which are necessary to ensure the health and performance of SQL Server. This chapter explores the functionality of SQL Server Agent, how it is used for job management, and best practices for leveraging its capabilities to optimize SQL Server administration.

SQL Server Agent is tightly integrated into SQL Server Management Studio (SSMS) and provides an intuitive interface for managing and scheduling jobs. A job in SQL Server Agent consists of one or more steps, with each step representing an individual task to be executed.

These steps can involve running Transact-SQL queries, executing operating system commands, or invoking PowerShell scripts. Administrators can create jobs for a wide range of tasks, from performing regular backups to running complex maintenance routines. By automating these processes, SQL Server Agent ensures that important tasks are carried out at the correct time, without the need for manual input, and helps to prevent the human errors that can arise from manual intervention.

Each job in SQL Server Agent can be customized with specific schedules and conditions. For example, a backup job may be set to run nightly, while a report generation job could be scheduled to run at the end of each week. Administrators can define multiple schedules for a single job or configure jobs to run in response to specific events, such as the completion of another job. This flexibility makes SQL Server Agent a powerful tool for managing both regular maintenance tasks and ad-hoc operations, such as data imports or large queries. The ability to create custom schedules for each job ensures that tasks are performed efficiently, and that the system's performance is not negatively impacted by concurrent operations.

Job steps are the individual actions that SQL Server Agent will execute as part of a job. A job can consist of one or more steps, each of which can run different types of commands. For instance, a step might involve running a backup command, executing a stored procedure, or running an external script. These steps can be configured to execute in sequence or in parallel, depending on the requirements of the task at hand. SQL Server Agent allows administrators to specify error-handling behaviors for each step, such as retrying a step on failure, proceeding to the next step even if a step fails, or stopping the job entirely if a step encounters an error. This level of control over job execution makes it possible to ensure that even complex tasks are completed successfully, without unexpected interruptions.

In addition to job steps, SQL Server Agent includes the concept of job schedules, which define when a job should be executed. A job can be scheduled to run at specific times, such as during off-peak hours, or to execute on a recurring basis. Schedules can be as simple as running a job once per day or as complex as running a job on a specific day of the week at a specific time. The ability to create flexible schedules is particularly useful for managing system resources, as administrators can ensure that resource-intensive tasks, such as backups and maintenance, run during periods of low database activity. By doing so, SQL Server Agent helps to balance workload demands and avoid performance degradation during peak usage times.

SQL Server Agent also provides built-in alerting and notification features that can help administrators track job execution and receive notifications when issues arise. For example, administrators can configure SQL Server Agent to send an email or write to the Windows Event Log when a job fails, completes successfully, or encounters a specific error condition. Alerts can be customized based on job status, error severity, or completion time, ensuring that administrators are immediately notified of critical issues. This functionality is particularly valuable in production environments where the timely resolution of problems is essential for minimizing downtime and maintaining database availability.

One of the most useful aspects of SQL Server Agent is its ability to execute jobs in response to specific events. SQL Server Agent can be configured to run jobs when certain conditions are met, such as the occurrence of a specific event or the completion of another job. For example, an administrator might configure a job to run a report generation process immediately after a data import job completes successfully. This event-driven execution helps to automate complex workflows, ensuring that tasks are executed in the correct order and that the system remains synchronized and efficient.

While SQL Server Agent is a powerful tool for automating administrative tasks, it is important for administrators to follow best practices to ensure that it is used effectively. One best practice is to regularly monitor job history and performance. SQL Server Agent keeps a log of job execution history, including the status of each job step, the duration of each step, and any error messages encountered during execution. By reviewing job history regularly, administrators can identify potential issues, such as recurring failures or long-running tasks, and take corrective action before these issues impact system performance.

Another best practice is to set appropriate job retention policies. Over time, SQL Server Agent stores large amounts of job history data, which can consume significant disk space if not managed properly. Administrators should configure SQL Server Agent to retain only the most recent job history entries, deleting older records to free up storage. This helps prevent job history logs from growing excessively and ensures that only relevant information is retained.

SQL Server Agent also provides a set of system-level jobs that run automatically, such as jobs for backup, index maintenance, and database integrity checks. These system jobs are critical for ensuring the health of SQL Server, and administrators should review them periodically to ensure that they are configured correctly and running as expected. Custom jobs can be created to supplement these system jobs, enabling administrators to tailor job execution to the specific needs of their environment. For example, an administrator might create a custom job to perform a database shrink operation or run a script to check for database fragmentation.

In environments with multiple SQL Server instances, SQL Server Agent can be configured to manage jobs across all instances from a central location. SQL Server Management Studio (SSMS) allows administrators to connect to multiple instances and view job status, history, and schedules for each server. This centralized management feature is particularly useful in large-scale environments where administrators need to manage a large number of SQL Server instances and ensure that jobs are executed consistently across the entire infrastructure.

SQL Server Agent also supports the use of proxies to execute jobs on behalf of users. A proxy is a security principal that allows SQL Server Agent to execute a job step using specific credentials, rather than relying on the SQL Server Agent service account. This feature is important for ensuring that jobs are executed securely, as it allows administrators to control which accounts can execute specific tasks and ensures that sensitive operations are performed under the appropriate security context.

SQL Server Agent and job management are vital for streamlining SQL Server administration and ensuring that critical tasks are performed on time and without error. By automating tasks such as backups, maintenance, and monitoring, SQL Server Agent reduces administrative overhead and improves system reliability. With the flexibility to configure job schedules, error handling, notifications, and event-driven executions, SQL Server Agent provides administrators with the tools needed to manage SQL Server instances efficiently and effectively. By following best practices for job management, monitoring job history, and utilizing built-in security features, administrators can optimize the use of SQL Server Agent and ensure that their database environments are running smoothly and securely.

# Configuring and Using SQL Server Profiler

SQL Server Profiler is a powerful tool that allows database administrators to capture and analyze SQL Server events and activity in real-time. This tool is invaluable for troubleshooting performance issues, monitoring queries, tracking the execution of SQL statements, and identifying bottlenecks or inefficiencies in the SQL Server environment. By capturing a detailed log of events, SQL Server Profiler provides deep insights into the internal workings of the database engine, making it possible to track query performance, diagnose errors, and understand the system's behavior under various workloads. This chapter explores how to configure and use SQL Server Profiler effectively, its various features, and best practices for leveraging its capabilities in both development and production environments.

SQL Server Profiler is essentially a graphical interface for working with SQL Server Trace, an underlying functionality that allows you to monitor the activity occurring within SQL Server. It is integrated into SQL Server Management Studio (SSMS), providing an accessible way to monitor and capture real-time SQL Server events. The tool captures a wide range of events, including SQL queries, stored procedure executions, user logins, and system errors, along with additional data such as execution duration, the number of rows affected, and the resource consumption associated with each event. These captured events are written to a trace file or displayed in the Profiler window, where they can be analyzed for performance optimization and troubleshooting.

To configure SQL Server Profiler, administrators first need to launch the tool from SQL Server Management Studio. Once opened, users can begin creating a new trace session. The process starts by defining the events that should be captured. SQL Server Profiler provides a set of predefined templates designed for different purposes, such as Tuning, Standard, and Replay. Each template includes a set of events and columns configured for a particular use case. For instance, the Tuning template is optimized for performance monitoring, capturing events like SQL statements, query duration, and resource usage. The Standard template captures a broader set of events that are useful for troubleshooting general issues. Administrators can also create custom templates to tailor the trace to specific needs, choosing from over 70 different event categories, such as query execution, lock management, and transaction handling.

After selecting the desired events, administrators can further refine the trace by choosing specific columns to capture, such as the duration of each query, the number of reads and writes, and the database context in which the query is executed. Profiler also allows for filtering, which enables users to limit the captured data to specific databases, applications, or user sessions. For example, an administrator can set up a trace to monitor only queries executed on a specific table or by a particular user. Filters help reduce the amount of data captured and make it easier to analyze specific behaviors, especially in environments with high levels of activity.

Once the trace is configured, SQL Server Profiler begins capturing events and displaying them in real time. The captured data is shown in a grid format, with each row representing a single event. Each event provides details such as the query text, the time it was executed, the duration of the execution, and any associated resource usage. This real-time capture makes it possible to quickly identify slow-running queries, long-duration transactions, and other performance issues. Profiler also includes a number of built-in analysis tools, such as the ability to calculate average query duration, view execution plans, and track deadlocks.

In addition to capturing real-time data, SQL Server Profiler allows administrators to save traces to files for later analysis. These trace files can be stored in a variety of formats, including SQL Server Trace, which is a binary format that can later be opened and analyzed in Profiler, or CSV files for easy import into other tools such as Excel for further analysis. Saving traces provides an audit trail of events, which can be useful for historical analysis, troubleshooting recurring issues, or conducting post-mortem reviews of performance incidents.

One of the key benefits of SQL Server Profiler is its ability to provide detailed information on query performance. By analyzing query duration and resource usage, administrators can identify slow-running queries, resource-intensive operations, and missing indexes. Profiler provides the execution duration of each query, which helps identify queries that are consuming excessive CPU or disk I/O. Long-running queries can often indicate inefficient query plans or missing indexes, and Profiler can be used to capture the execution plan of a query, allowing administrators to see how SQL Server is processing the query and which steps are causing delays.

Additionally, SQL Server Profiler can capture deadlock events, which occur when two or more transactions are blocked indefinitely, each waiting for the other to release locks. Deadlocks are one of the most common causes of performance issues in SQL Server, and identifying them is crucial for resolving resource contention problems. Profiler provides a detailed deadlock graph, which visually represents the chain of events that led to the deadlock, including the SQL statements involved and the resources that were locked. This graphical representation makes it easier to understand and resolve deadlocks, helping to optimize query performance and prevent future occurrences.

While SQL Server Profiler is an invaluable tool for diagnosing performance issues, it is important to use it judiciously, especially in production environments. Capturing all SQL Server activity can create a significant performance overhead, particularly on busy servers with high transaction volumes. Running a trace for extended periods can slow down query execution and consume system resources, potentially causing the very performance issues being investigated. Therefore, it is best to use SQL Server Profiler for short intervals and target specific issues or patterns. Administrators should also be mindful of the data retention settings and ensure that captured trace files are properly stored and managed to prevent them from consuming excessive disk space.

For long-term monitoring and less resource-intensive alternatives, administrators can use Extended Events, a lightweight, more efficient event-tracking system in SQL Server. While SQL Server Profiler is ideal for short-term diagnostics and ad-hoc analysis, Extended Events offer a more scalable solution for ongoing performance monitoring, especially in production environments. Extended Events allow administrators to capture and store event data without significantly impacting system performance. Extended Events also provide greater flexibility in terms of filtering, grouping, and handling event data.

Despite the availability of Extended Events, SQL Server Profiler remains an essential tool for capturing a broad range of events in real-time and analyzing detailed query performance. The tool's ability to display live data and capture extensive information about SQL queries, server activities, and system resources makes it an indispensable part of a DBA's toolkit. When used appropriately, SQL Server Profiler can help identify performance bottlenecks, optimize queries, and resolve complex issues that would otherwise be difficult to diagnose.

In summary, SQL Server Profiler is a powerful diagnostic tool that provides deep insights into SQL Server activity. By capturing and analyzing a wide range of events, administrators can monitor query performance, identify resource-intensive operations, track deadlocks, and troubleshoot issues in real time. While Profiler is an invaluable tool for performance analysis, it should be used with care in production environments to avoid unnecessary overhead. With careful configuration and monitoring, SQL Server Profiler can significantly enhance the ability of database administrators to optimize SQL Server performance and ensure the smooth operation of the database system.

# Advanced Database Maintenance and Integrity Checks

Database maintenance is a critical aspect of managing SQL Server environments, as it ensures the ongoing health, performance, and reliability of the system. SQL Server databases require regular maintenance to perform efficiently, and it is essential to not only address day-to-day administrative tasks like backups and index optimization but also to perform more advanced maintenance activities that help maintain data integrity, ensure system stability, and optimize performance. These advanced maintenance techniques are designed to prevent issues before they occur, detect hidden problems, and improve the long-term performance and reliability of the database system. This chapter explores some of the advanced database maintenance and integrity check strategies that SQL Server administrators should consider incorporating into their maintenance routines.

One of the foundational aspects of SQL Server maintenance is ensuring that the database's integrity is preserved. SQL Server databases can become corrupted over time due to various factors such as hardware failures, software bugs, or unexpected shutdowns. To mitigate these risks, administrators should regularly perform database consistency checks using the DBCC CHECKDB command. This command checks for any physical or logical inconsistencies within the database, such as corruption in database pages, missing or incorrect indexes, and broken relationships between data. DBCC CHECKDB is an important tool for detecting corruption early before it can cause data loss or system instability. By scheduling regular runs of DBCC CHECKDB, administrators can proactively identify and resolve issues before they escalate.

In addition to performing basic integrity checks, DBCC CHECKDB can also be used with specific options to target certain types of issues. For example, administrators can run DBCC CHECKDB with the NOINDEX option to check for corruption in the data pages while excluding the check on indexes. This can be helpful when a database contains a large number of indexes and performing a full integrity check would be too resource-intensive. Another option is DBCC CHECKDB with the

REPAIR_ALLOW_DATA_LOSS command, which attempts to repair detected corruption, though it is important to note that this command may result in some data loss. Therefore, administrators should always ensure that they have a full, recent backup before using this option.

Index fragmentation is another common issue that can impact SQL Server performance. Fragmentation occurs when the logical order of data pages in an index does not match the physical order, leading to inefficient data retrieval and increased I/O operations. Over time, as records are inserted, updated, and deleted, indexes can become fragmented, causing query performance to degrade. SQL Server provides two primary commands for addressing index fragmentation: DBCC INDEXDEFRAG and ALTER INDEX. While DBCC INDEXDEFRAG is an older command that can be used to reorganize fragmented indexes, it is now recommended to use the ALTER INDEX REORGANIZE or REBUILD options for better control and efficiency.

Rebuilding indexes is a more effective way to address fragmentation, as it essentially drops and recreates the index, resulting in a completely defragmented structure. This process can be resource-intensive, however, and may cause performance issues if done during peak usage times. Administrators should consider scheduling index rebuilds during off-peak hours or during a maintenance window. The ALTER INDEX REBUILD command can also be used with options to optimize the rebuild process, such as rebuilding only those indexes that have reached a certain level of fragmentation, thus reducing unnecessary work. Regularly rebuilding or reorganizing indexes can help maintain SQL Server performance, especially in databases with frequent updates or heavy write workloads.

In addition to index optimization, maintaining up-to-date statistics is crucial for ensuring that SQL Server queries execute efficiently. SQL Server uses statistics to determine the most optimal query execution plan, and outdated or missing statistics can lead to inefficient query plans, longer execution times, and excessive resource usage. Administrators should schedule regular updates of statistics using the UPDATE STATISTICS command or use the sp_updatestats stored procedure to automatically update statistics for all tables in the database. While SQL Server automatically updates statistics in certain cases, it is recommended to perform manual updates periodically, especially for large databases with high transaction volumes or frequently changing data.

Database backups are an essential part of database maintenance, but they are also an area where more advanced practices can greatly enhance the resilience and recoverability of the system. SQL Server offers a variety of backup options, including full, differential, and transaction log backups. While a full backup captures the entire database, a differential backup only includes the changes since the last full backup, and a transaction log backup includes all transaction logs that have occurred since the last log backup. Using a combination of these backup types ensures that databases can be restored to any point in time and minimizes the risk of data loss.

Advanced backup strategies involve more than just creating periodic backups. SQL Server administrators should implement backup verification techniques, such as running DBCC CHECKDB after each restore operation to ensure that the backup file is not corrupted. Administrators should also consider implementing backup compression to reduce the amount of disk space required for backups and improve backup performance. Additionally, it is important to establish a clear backup retention policy, determining how long backups will be kept, which backups will be retained for disaster recovery purposes, and which can be archived or discarded.

Another important maintenance activity is monitoring and managing SQL Server's system resources, including disk space, memory, and CPU. Over time, databases grow, and so do the system's resource requirements. Without proper monitoring and resource allocation, SQL Server can experience performance degradation, especially if it runs out of disk space or memory. SQL Server provides dynamic management views (DMVs) to help administrators monitor resource usage, such as sys.dm_exec_requests for tracking active queries and sys.dm_os_performance_counters for monitoring memory and CPU usage. By regularly reviewing these metrics, administrators can identify resource bottlenecks and address them proactively.

Disk space management is particularly crucial when dealing with large databases. Administrators should ensure that sufficient disk space is available for data and log files, and that these files are not fragmented or growing uncontrollably. SQL Server provides the sys.dm_db_file_space_usage DMV to track disk space usage within a database, helping administrators ensure that storage is properly allocated and avoid running out of space unexpectedly. Disk space should also be managed in conjunction with tempdb, as it can grow rapidly during large query executions or bulk operations.

Performing integrity checks and maintenance tasks not only ensures the health of the database but also helps with the system's security posture. Security patches, updates, and vulnerability assessments should be regularly performed to protect against external threats. This includes managing database user permissions, auditing access logs, and ensuring that sensitive data is properly encrypted or masked. Advanced security maintenance tasks also involve configuring and managing SQL Server's built-in security features, such as Transparent Data Encryption (TDE) and auditing tools, to safeguard data both in transit and at rest.

By incorporating advanced database maintenance and integrity checks into regular SQL Server management routines, administrators can ensure that the database remains stable, secure, and efficient. These practices not only reduce the likelihood of performance degradation and data corruption but also provide the necessary tools for proactively managing SQL Server environments. Regularly performing integrity checks, optimizing indexes, maintaining up-to-date statistics, and following a comprehensive backup strategy are essential steps in ensuring that SQL Server remains reliable and capable of supporting the demanding needs of modern businesses.

# Implementing SQL Server High Availability Solutions

High availability (HA) is a critical requirement for modern SQL Server environments, where business operations rely heavily on the continuous availability of data. SQL Server high availability solutions ensure that database services are available even during hardware failures, system crashes, or other unexpected events. Achieving high availability involves using various technologies and techniques to minimize downtime, provide redundancy, and ensure data integrity. This chapter explores different SQL Server high availability solutions, including AlwaysOn Availability Groups, failover clustering, database mirroring, and log shipping, as well as how to implement them to provide a robust and resilient SQL Server environment.

One of the most powerful and flexible high availability solutions available in SQL Server is AlwaysOn Availability Groups, introduced in SQL Server 2012. AlwaysOn Availability Groups enable high availability by replicating databases across multiple SQL Server instances, ensuring that a copy of the database is always available in the event of a failure. The primary replica is the server that handles read-write operations, while secondary replicas contain read-only copies of the database. These secondary replicas can be used for read-only queries, offloading some of the workload from the primary replica and improving performance.

AlwaysOn Availability Groups support automatic failover, meaning that if the primary replica fails, one of the secondary replicas is automatically promoted to become the new primary replica, ensuring minimal downtime. The availability group can have multiple secondary replicas, and each replica can be configured to support either synchronous or asynchronous replication. In synchronous mode, the transaction is committed to both the primary and secondary replicas simultaneously, ensuring that no data is lost in the event of a failover. However, synchronous replication can introduce some latency, especially in geographically distributed environments. Asynchronous replication, on the other hand, allows the primary replica to commit transactions without waiting for the secondary replica, which can improve performance but may introduce the risk of data loss during failover if the secondary replica is behind.

To implement AlwaysOn Availability Groups, administrators must configure Windows Server Failover Clustering (WSFC), which is the underlying infrastructure that manages the health and status of the SQL Server instances in the availability group. WSFC monitors the availability of SQL Server instances and handles automatic failover when a failure is detected. The configuration of AlwaysOn Availability Groups also requires the setup of a listener, which provides a single point of contact for clients, allowing them to connect to the availability group without worrying about which replica is currently active.

Failover clustering is another high availability solution in SQL Server that provides redundancy at the server level, rather than the database level. In a SQL Server failover cluster, multiple physical servers are grouped together into a cluster, with one active node and one or more passive nodes. The active node is where SQL Server runs, and the passive nodes are on standby, ready to take over if the active node fails. When a failure occurs, the SQL Server instance is automatically moved to one of the passive nodes, ensuring that the database remains available with minimal downtime.

Failover clustering provides high availability for all databases on the clustered SQL Server instance, as the entire instance, including all databases, is failed over. However, unlike AlwaysOn Availability Groups, failover clustering does not allow for read-only replicas or fine-grained control over which databases are included in the failover process. Additionally, failover clustering requires shared storage, such as a Storage Area Network (SAN), to ensure that all nodes in the cluster can access the same database files. While failover clustering provides strong fault tolerance, it can be more complex to configure and maintain, particularly in larger environments.

Database mirroring is a legacy high availability solution that was introduced in SQL Server 2005 and remains available in some editions of SQL Server. In database mirroring, changes made to a primary database are mirrored to a secondary database on a separate SQL Server instance. Like AlwaysOn Availability Groups, database mirroring supports automatic failover, with a witness server that monitors the health of the primary and mirrored servers. If the primary server fails, the witness server automatically promotes the mirrored server to become the new primary. Database mirroring supports both high-safety mode (synchronous replication) and high-performance mode (asynchronous replication).

While database mirroring is a useful high availability solution, it is somewhat limited compared to AlwaysOn Availability Groups. For instance, database mirroring only supports a single database, while AlwaysOn Availability Groups can handle multiple databases in a single availability group. Additionally, database mirroring does not allow for read-only replicas, limiting its ability to offload read queries from the primary server. Database mirroring has also been deprecated in newer versions of SQL Server in favor of AlwaysOn Availability Groups, which offer more advanced features and better scalability.

Log shipping is another method for achieving high availability in SQL Server, although it is not as sophisticated as AlwaysOn Availability Groups or failover clustering. Log shipping involves periodically backing up the transaction logs of a primary database, copying them to a secondary server, and applying the logs to a secondary copy of the database. This ensures that the secondary database is kept up to date with the primary database, providing redundancy and disaster recovery capabilities. In the event of a failure on the primary server, the secondary database can be brought online by applying the most recent transaction log backups.

While log shipping provides basic high availability, it has several limitations. The failover process is not automatic, meaning that administrators must manually promote the secondary server in the event of a failure. Additionally, log shipping does not support real-time replication, and there may be a delay between when a change is made to the primary database and when it is replicated to the secondary database. Log shipping is best suited for environments where occasional failover is acceptable, and where real-time data replication is not a critical requirement.

SQL Server also offers a range of additional high availability features, such as AlwaysOn Failover Cluster Instances (FCIs), which combine failover clustering with AlwaysOn Availability Groups to provide even higher levels of redundancy and availability. FCIs provide automatic failover at the instance level, ensuring that the entire SQL Server instance is available on a secondary node in the event of a failure. By combining FCIs with Availability Groups, administrators can achieve both high availability and disaster recovery in a single configuration.

In addition to implementing high availability solutions, administrators must also focus on proper monitoring and maintenance to ensure the ongoing health and availability of the SQL Server environment. Regularly monitoring the status of replicas, checking for replication latency, and verifying that failover processes are functioning correctly are all critical aspects of high availability management. Administrators should also perform regular backups and ensure that backup strategies are in place for all replicas, including secondary replicas, to ensure that data can be recovered in the event of a failure.

In a modern SQL Server environment, high availability is essential to ensure that applications and services remain accessible and reliable. Whether using AlwaysOn Availability Groups, failover clustering, database mirroring, or log shipping, implementing a high availability solution requires careful planning, configuration, and monitoring to ensure that the system remains resilient to failures. By choosing the right high availability solution and maintaining best practices for monitoring and maintenance, organizations can ensure that their SQL Server instances remain available, secure, and performant, even in the face of hardware failures or other disruptions.

# Disaster Recovery Planning and Strategies

Disaster recovery planning is an essential component of any robust IT infrastructure, particularly for SQL Server environments where data is a critical asset. A disaster recovery plan (DRP) defines the processes, strategies, and procedures that organizations use to recover from unexpected events such as hardware failures, software bugs, cyber-attacks, or natural disasters. The objective is to minimize downtime, ensure data integrity, and restore services as quickly as possible. For SQL Server environments, a comprehensive disaster recovery strategy should address data availability, backup strategies, failover systems, and the recovery of databases and other critical services in the event of a disaster. This chapter explores the key aspects of disaster recovery planning for SQL Server, outlining strategies for data protection, failover systems, backup and restoration techniques, and more.

The first step in creating a disaster recovery plan is understanding the key components that need to be protected. For SQL Server, this primarily involves ensuring that the database and associated data files are backed up and can be restored in the event of failure. This includes full databases, transaction logs, and system configurations such as SQL

Server settings and user accounts. The data itself is the most critical component, as it represents the core of SQL Server's operations, but the system's configuration, including SQL Server Agent jobs, linked servers, and other administrative settings, must also be preserved to ensure a full and accurate recovery.

Backup strategies are at the heart of any disaster recovery plan. SQL Server offers several types of backups, each serving a different purpose: full backups, differential backups, transaction log backups, and file and filegroup backups. Full backups capture the entire database, including all data and objects. Differential backups capture only the changes made since the last full backup, making them smaller and faster to create than full backups. Transaction log backups record all the transaction log changes that have occurred since the last log backup, allowing for point-in-time recovery and ensuring that no data is lost between full or differential backups. File and filegroup backups provide a way to back up specific files or parts of a database, allowing for more granular recovery.

A critical aspect of backup strategy is defining a proper backup schedule. Depending on the organization's data change rate, transaction volume, and recovery point objectives (RPO), backups should be scheduled at regular intervals to ensure that data is protected without putting unnecessary strain on system resources. Transaction log backups, for instance, should be taken frequently—often every 15 to 30 minutes—to minimize the risk of data loss. Full and differential backups should be scheduled at appropriate intervals, taking into account both the size of the database and the acceptable level of downtime.

For a disaster recovery plan to be effective, backups need to be properly managed. Storing backups in multiple locations is crucial for preventing data loss. On-site backups provide quick recovery in case of a failure, but off-site backups offer additional protection in the event of a site-wide disaster, such as a fire or flood. Cloud storage has become an increasingly popular option for off-site backups due to its scalability, security, and ease of access. Cloud backup solutions allow organizations to store large amounts of backup data and access it from anywhere, making them ideal for distributed environments. Furthermore, it is essential that backups are regularly tested and validated to ensure that they can be restored when needed. Administrators should routinely perform test restores to verify the integrity of backup files and confirm that the restoration process is smooth and efficient.

Another key strategy in disaster recovery is ensuring high availability through failover systems. SQL Server provides several options for high availability, including AlwaysOn Availability Groups, failover clustering, and database mirroring. These systems allow for automatic or manual failover to a secondary server or replica in the event of a primary server failure. AlwaysOn Availability Groups, for example, provide automatic failover between replicas, which can be either synchronous or asynchronous, ensuring that one replica always remains available. Failover clustering operates at the instance level, meaning that the entire SQL Server instance is moved to a secondary node in case of failure, while database mirroring replicates a single database to a mirror server, allowing for fast failover with minimal data loss.

Using high availability solutions in tandem with backup strategies allows for a more comprehensive disaster recovery plan. While backups are essential for data protection and recovery, failover systems ensure that the application remains available during the recovery process, minimizing downtime and impact on users. By using technologies like AlwaysOn Availability Groups and failover clustering, SQL Server administrators can achieve near-zero downtime, ensuring that users can continue to access the database even in the event of hardware failures or other disruptions.

When implementing a disaster recovery strategy for SQL Server, it is also important to define clear recovery objectives. These include the recovery point objective (RPO), which specifies the acceptable amount of data loss in the event of a failure, and the recovery time objective (RTO), which defines the maximum amount of time allowed for database recovery. Organizations should assess the criticality of their SQL Server workloads and decide on the appropriate backup frequency, failover solutions, and recovery procedures based on these objectives. For example, a highly transactional database that requires continuous availability may use AlwaysOn Availability Groups with synchronous replication and frequent transaction log backups to minimize data loss and downtime.

Additionally, administrators must develop a plan for restoring SQL Server to its pre-disaster state. The recovery process involves restoring the most recent backup, applying any transaction log backups to bring the database up to the point of failure, and reconfiguring SQL Server settings as needed. Restoring large databases can take considerable time, depending on the size of the backups and the speed of the recovery infrastructure. To expedite recovery, administrators should ensure that they have a well-documented recovery procedure, complete with step-by-step instructions for restoring SQL Server, applying backups, and verifying the integrity of the recovered data.

Testing the disaster recovery plan is also crucial. Regularly testing the plan helps ensure that the recovery procedures are effective and that the IT staff is familiar with the process. Disaster recovery testing should include both simulated failovers and the restoration of backups to ensure that the recovery time objective (RTO) and recovery point objective (RPO) are met. Testing helps identify any weaknesses in the plan, such as slow recovery times or missing data, so that improvements can be made before an actual disaster occurs. It is also important to test failover systems, backup restores, and the performance of recovered databases under real-world conditions.

In summary, disaster recovery planning is a vital component of managing SQL Server environments. A robust disaster recovery strategy involves a combination of regular backups, high availability solutions, and comprehensive recovery processes. By implementing advanced backup and high availability solutions, defining clear recovery objectives, and regularly testing the disaster recovery plan, organizations can ensure that their SQL Server environments remain resilient to failures, minimize downtime, and protect critical business data. Having a well-structured disaster recovery plan in place enables organizations to respond quickly to unexpected disruptions and maintain continuous database availability.

# SQL Server Performance Monitoring Tools

SQL Server performance monitoring is a critical aspect of database administration, as it enables administrators to track system health, diagnose issues, and optimize performance. Effective monitoring helps to ensure that SQL Server instances are running efficiently and that resources are being used appropriately. SQL Server provides a range of performance monitoring tools that allow administrators to gather real-time data, analyze performance metrics, and proactively address potential issues before they impact users. These tools provide insight into various aspects of SQL Server performance, including CPU usage, memory consumption, disk I/O, query execution, and more. This chapter delves into the primary performance monitoring tools available in SQL Server and how they can be leveraged to maintain a healthy database environment.

One of the most widely used tools for monitoring SQL Server performance is SQL Server Management Studio (SSMS), which includes several built-in features for tracking performance. SSMS provides a graphical interface that allows administrators to easily monitor various aspects of SQL Server performance, such as the health of databases, query performance, and resource utilization. SSMS includes several predefined reports that provide insights into common performance issues. These reports offer an overview of key performance indicators (KPIs), including CPU usage, memory usage, disk space, and query performance.

SQL Server Profiler is another powerful tool that helps administrators capture and analyze SQL Server events in real time. Profiler allows for the detailed tracking of SQL queries, stored procedures, transactions, and other SQL Server activities. It is particularly useful for identifying performance bottlenecks, slow-running queries, and resource-intensive operations. Administrators can use Profiler to capture events related to query execution times, the number of rows affected, and the type of operations being performed. SQL Server Profiler can be configured to filter events based on specific criteria, such as query type, database name, or user session, allowing administrators to focus on areas that require optimization.

For more advanced and less resource-intensive monitoring, SQL Server also offers Dynamic Management Views (DMVs), which provide real-time data on SQL Server performance. DMVs are a set of system views that expose a wide range of internal information about SQL Server's state, including details on system resources, query execution, and database health. DMVs can be queried to monitor CPU usage, memory consumption, disk I/O, blocking, and query performance, among other metrics. For example, sys.dm_exec_requests provides information on currently running queries, while sys.dm_exec_query_stats offers statistics on the execution of queries over time. These views are an invaluable tool for diagnosing performance issues and identifying which queries or processes are consuming the most resources.

The Performance Monitor (PerfMon) tool in Windows is another useful resource for monitoring SQL Server performance. While not specific to SQL Server, PerfMon allows administrators to track system-level performance metrics such as CPU usage, memory usage, disk activity, and network traffic. PerfMon provides a granular view of system performance by allowing administrators to monitor individual counters related to SQL Server, such as SQL Server's buffer cache hit ratio or the number of disk read and write operations. PerfMon can be used alongside SQL Server-specific tools like Profiler and DMVs to give a more comprehensive view of how SQL Server interacts with the underlying operating system and hardware resources.

SQL Server Management Data Warehouse (MDW) is another tool designed for advanced performance monitoring and reporting. MDW collects performance data over time, providing long-term insights into how SQL Server is performing and helping administrators identify trends, recurring issues, or potential areas for improvement. MDW can be configured to collect data on a wide range of SQL Server metrics, including query execution, server health, and resource utilization. The collected data is stored in a dedicated database, where it can be queried and analyzed using predefined reports or custom queries. MDW is particularly useful for administrators who need to monitor SQL Server performance over extended periods or across multiple servers.

Extended Events (XEvents) is a lightweight, flexible event-tracing system in SQL Server that can be used for performance monitoring. Extended Events provide a more efficient and scalable alternative to

SQL Server Profiler, especially in environments with high transaction volumes or large amounts of event data. XEvents allows administrators to capture and filter events related to SQL Server performance, such as query execution, blocking, deadlocks, and resource consumption. XEvents are highly configurable and can be used to monitor specific server behaviors or track performance metrics over time. One of the key advantages of Extended Events is its low overhead, as it uses minimal system resources, making it ideal for production environments.

Another important tool for SQL Server performance monitoring is the Query Store, which was introduced in SQL Server 2016. Query Store captures historical query performance data and execution plans, allowing administrators to track and analyze the performance of queries over time. It is particularly useful for diagnosing performance regressions, as it helps identify when a query's performance began to degrade and what changes might have caused the issue. Query Store provides detailed information about query execution, including the number of executions, execution duration, and the execution plan used. It also allows administrators to force a particular execution plan, which can help resolve performance issues caused by changes in query plans due to parameter sniffing or query optimization.

Resource Governor is another important tool in SQL Server that can help monitor and control resource usage. Resource Governor allows administrators to define resource pools and workload groups, enabling fine-grained control over how CPU, memory, and I/O resources are allocated to different SQL Server workloads. By configuring Resource Governor, administrators can prioritize critical workloads, such as transaction processing, and ensure that less important workloads, such as reporting queries, do not consume excessive resources. This tool helps prevent resource contention and ensures that SQL Server operates efficiently, even under heavy workloads.

In addition to these tools, SQL Server also provides various diagnostic and troubleshooting features for monitoring performance. SQL Server provides error logs, event logs, and system logs that can be reviewed for signs of performance issues or system failures. SQL Server also includes a variety of diagnostic stored procedures that can be run to gather additional information about server performance, including sys.dm_exec_sessions for tracking active sessions and sys.dm_exec_query_plan for analyzing query execution plans. These tools can be used in conjunction with other performance monitoring tools to provide a comprehensive picture of SQL Server health and performance.

To get the most out of SQL Server's performance monitoring tools, it is essential to establish a proactive monitoring strategy. This involves regularly reviewing performance metrics, setting up automated alerts for critical conditions (such as high CPU usage or excessive blocking), and performing routine analysis to identify trends or potential issues. By combining SQL Server's built-in monitoring tools with external monitoring solutions, administrators can create a robust monitoring framework that ensures the SQL Server environment runs smoothly, efficiently, and without interruptions.

Effective SQL Server performance monitoring is essential for ensuring that SQL Server environments perform optimally and that potential issues are detected and addressed before they impact users. SQL Server provides a wide range of tools and features for monitoring and analyzing performance, including SQL Server Profiler, DMVs, Performance Monitor, Extended Events, Query Store, and Resource Governor. By understanding how these tools work and how to use them effectively, administrators can ensure that SQL Server operates at peak performance, providing a reliable and responsive environment for users and applications.

# Understanding SQL Server Query Plans

SQL Server query plans are essential for understanding how SQL Server executes queries. A query plan, also known as an execution plan, is a set of steps that SQL Server follows to retrieve the required data for a query. Understanding query plans is a vital skill for database administrators (DBAs) and developers because it provides deep insight into the performance of SQL queries, helping to identify bottlenecks and inefficiencies. Query plans not only show the sequence of operations that SQL Server will perform but also reveal how resources such as CPU, memory, and disk I/O are utilized during query execution. This chapter explores the structure of SQL Server query plans, how to interpret them, and how to use this information to optimize query performance.

At a high level, a query plan is generated by the SQL Server query optimizer, which analyzes the query and determines the most efficient way to execute it. The query optimizer evaluates various strategies based on factors such as available indexes, join methods, and statistics about the data distribution. It then selects the plan that it believes will execute the query most efficiently, minimizing resource usage and execution time. However, the optimizer does not always choose the optimal plan, particularly in complex queries or situations where statistics are outdated or missing. As such, DBAs must be able to read and interpret query plans to ensure optimal query performance.

A SQL Server query plan can be visualized in two main formats: a graphical execution plan and a text-based execution plan. The graphical execution plan is the most commonly used format in SQL Server Management Studio (SSMS) and is useful for visualizing the steps involved in query execution. This format uses icons and arrows to represent the operations, making it easier to follow the flow of data through the query. The text-based execution plan, on the other hand, is a detailed, row-by-row breakdown of the operations and their costs, which can be viewed in the execution plan tab of SSMS or captured using a T-SQL command.

The graphical execution plan displays a series of operators connected by arrows, where each operator represents a specific action or operation SQL Server performs on the data. For example, the "Table Scan" operator indicates that SQL Server is scanning an entire table to retrieve the requested data, while an "Index Seek" operator indicates that SQL Server is using an index to locate specific rows. Each operator has an associated cost, which represents the amount of resources (such as CPU time, I/O, and memory) required to perform that operation. The cost is typically displayed as a percentage, with the most resource-intensive operations appearing first. DBAs can use this information to identify which steps in the query are consuming the most resources and to focus optimization efforts on those operations.

In a graphical plan, the flow of data is represented by arrows that connect the operators. These arrows indicate the movement of data between the different steps in the query execution. For example, data may flow from a table scan to a join operator, or from a sort operator to an output step. By following the arrows, DBAs can trace how SQL Server is processing the query and understand the flow of data through the various stages of the execution plan.

The text-based execution plan, while more detailed, can be harder to interpret due to its verbosity. This plan provides a step-by-step breakdown of the operations involved in executing the query, including the estimated number of rows processed at each step and the cost of each operation. The text-based plan is especially useful for advanced troubleshooting and optimization, as it provides more granular information than the graphical plan. However, interpreting the text-based plan requires a solid understanding of SQL Server internals and query execution strategies.

A key part of query optimization is identifying and addressing inefficient query plans. One common problem that can appear in query plans is the use of a "Table Scan" operator. A table scan occurs when SQL Server must read every row in a table to find the requested data. Table scans can be slow, especially for large tables, and often indicate that an index is missing or poorly designed. In contrast, an "Index Seek" operator, which indicates that SQL Server is using an index to locate the requested rows, is typically much faster than a table scan, as it allows SQL Server to jump directly to the relevant data.

Another common issue in query plans is the use of inefficient join methods. SQL Server uses several different join algorithms, including nested loops, hash joins, and merge joins. The optimizer selects the join method based on factors such as the size of the tables being joined, the availability of indexes, and the data distribution. In some cases, the optimizer may choose a suboptimal join method that results in poor performance. For example, a hash join may be chosen for two small tables, even though a merge join would be more efficient. By reviewing the query plan, DBAs can determine whether the chosen join method is appropriate and consider rewriting the query or adjusting indexes to improve performance.

One of the most important elements in query plans is the cost associated with each operation. The cost represents the estimated resource usage for each step in the query. High-cost operations indicate areas where the query can be optimized. For example, if the query involves a sort operation, and the cost is high, it may be a sign that adding an index on the relevant columns could reduce the need for sorting. Similarly, if a join operation has a high cost, it may suggest that the query could be optimized by improving the join condition or ensuring that the appropriate indexes are in place.

One technique that DBAs can use to optimize query performance is index tuning. SQL Server query plans often reveal whether indexes are being used efficiently or whether queries are performing full table scans. If a query is not using an index as expected, the query plan can help identify which index might be appropriate. In some cases, adding a new index or modifying an existing one can significantly improve query performance. DBAs should regularly monitor query plans to ensure that indexes are being used effectively and to identify opportunities for index optimization.

Another important aspect of query plan optimization is statistics. SQL Server uses statistics to estimate the number of rows returned by each operation in the query plan. If the statistics are outdated or inaccurate, the optimizer may make poor decisions about the most efficient execution plan. It is important to ensure that statistics are regularly updated, especially after significant changes to the data. Administrators can use the UPDATE STATISTICS command or enable the AUTO_UPDATE_STATISTICS option to ensure that SQL Server maintains up-to-date statistics.

Understanding SQL Server query plans is essential for diagnosing performance problems and optimizing queries. By interpreting query plans, administrators can identify inefficient operations, such as table scans, unnecessary sorts, or suboptimal join methods, and take steps to optimize them. The information in query plans can also guide decisions about index design, statistics maintenance, and query rewriting. Regular analysis of query plans is a crucial part of maintaining high performance in SQL Server environments, ensuring that queries run efficiently and use system resources effectively.

# SQL Server Data Compression Techniques

SQL Server offers various techniques to optimize data storage, and one of the most effective methods for improving space utilization is data compression. Data compression allows organizations to reduce the amount of storage required for their SQL Server databases, leading to significant cost savings and improved system performance. By reducing the size of database tables and indexes, SQL Server data compression also helps to decrease I/O usage, improve query performance, and reduce backup and restore times. Understanding how data compression works in SQL Server, the types of compression available, and when to use them is crucial for database administrators (DBAs) seeking to optimize storage and system efficiency.

SQL Server supports two primary types of data compression: row-level compression and page-level compression. Row-level compression reduces the storage requirements of individual rows by eliminating unnecessary or redundant data storage. It works by minimizing the space used for fixed-length data types such as integers and dates, as well as variable-length data types like strings. Row-level compression is particularly effective for reducing the storage requirements of tables with many nullable columns or columns that contain repeated values. For example, in a column that contains a lot of NULL or zero values, row-level compression stores the absence of data more efficiently than the full data value would be.

Page-level compression, on the other hand, is more sophisticated and involves compressing entire data pages. SQL Server organizes data into 8KB pages, and page-level compression works by applying compression algorithms to these pages, reducing the overall storage required for large tables or indexes. Page-level compression is particularly useful for large databases with repetitive data or tables that contain a significant number of similar values across rows. The page-level compression algorithm uses techniques such as prefix and dictionary compression, which can achieve higher compression ratios than row-level compression alone. In some cases, page-level compression can reduce the size of a table or index by up to 50%, making it highly beneficial for space-constrained environments.

Both row-level and page-level compression are implemented using the SQL Server Data Compression feature, which can be enabled at the table or index level. Enabling compression on a table or index involves using the ALTER TABLE or ALTER INDEX command with the WITH (DATA_COMPRESSION = ROW) or WITH (DATA_COMPRESSION = PAGE) option. The choice between row and page compression depends on the specific characteristics of the data and the performance goals of the database. Row-level compression is generally more efficient for smaller datasets, while page-level compression is better suited for larger tables and indexes where the savings in disk space can be more substantial.

One of the key benefits of data compression is the reduction in I/O operations. When SQL Server retrieves compressed data from disk, it reads less data into memory, which can improve query performance, especially for large tables with many columns. By reducing the amount of data that needs to be read from disk and transferred to memory, data compression can reduce I/O latency and improve the overall performance of SQL queries. This is particularly beneficial for queries that involve full table scans, aggregations, or complex joins, as it reduces the amount of data that needs to be processed. However, while compression can improve query performance by reducing I/O, it can introduce some additional CPU overhead due to the compression and decompression processes. As such, administrators must balance the benefits of compression against the potential performance impact on CPU usage.

Data compression also has a significant impact on backup and restore operations. Compressed data reduces the amount of space required for backups, which can result in faster backup times and reduced storage costs for backup files. Compressed backups are especially beneficial in environments with large databases, as they reduce the time required to back up and restore data. Additionally, compressed backups reduce the storage requirements for backup files, making it easier to manage and retain multiple backup versions. However, it is important to note that compressed backups can incur additional CPU overhead during the backup and restore processes, and administrators should consider the trade-offs when deciding whether to use compression for backup purposes.

Another advantage of SQL Server data compression is the ability to optimize storage on disk. By reducing the size of tables and indexes, data compression helps organizations maximize the use of available storage resources. This can be particularly valuable in environments with limited disk capacity or where storage costs are a concern. In some cases, data compression can help organizations avoid the need to purchase additional storage by reducing the amount of space required for database files. Moreover, data compression can extend the lifespan of existing storage hardware by reducing the wear and tear caused by excessive disk I/O.

Despite its many benefits, data compression is not suitable for every scenario. For example, highly transactional tables with frequent updates may not benefit as much from compression, as the overhead of compressing and decompressing data during write operations can outweigh the benefits. Similarly, certain data types, such as already compressed binary data or media files, may not benefit from SQL Server's compression techniques. In these cases, administrators should carefully assess the impact of compression before applying it to such tables or indexes.

SQL Server provides a number of tools to help administrators assess the impact of data compression on their environment. The sp_estimate_data_compression_savings stored procedure allows administrators to estimate the potential savings in space when applying compression to a table or index. This can be useful for determining whether compression is likely to result in significant space savings before actually implementing it. Additionally, SQL Server's DATA_COMPRESSION options provide insight into the cost-benefit analysis of compression, allowing administrators to choose the most appropriate level of compression for their workload.

To get the most out of SQL Server data compression, administrators should also consider the maintenance implications. Compression can cause fragmentation in tables and indexes over time, especially in environments with high transaction rates. As a result, administrators may need to periodically reorganize or rebuild compressed indexes to maintain optimal performance. SQL Server provides several tools for managing index fragmentation, including the ALTER INDEX REORGANIZE and ALTER INDEX REBUILD commands. These tools help to optimize the structure of indexes, ensuring that data remains efficiently organized even after compression is applied.

In addition, administrators should regularly monitor the performance impact of compression and ensure that the system's CPU usage and memory resources are not adversely affected. Although data compression can reduce I/O and storage usage, it does introduce additional overhead, particularly during write operations. Monitoring tools such as SQL Server's Dynamic Management Views (DMVs) and the Resource Governor can help administrators track the CPU and memory usage associated with compression and adjust resource allocation as needed.

SQL Server's data compression techniques are powerful tools for optimizing storage, improving performance, and reducing the costs associated with managing large databases. By carefully assessing the benefits and potential drawbacks of compression, administrators can make informed decisions about when and where to apply compression within their SQL Server environment. With the ability to reduce disk space usage, optimize backups, and enhance query performance, data compression is a vital tool for maintaining efficient, high-performance SQL Server environments.

# SQL Server Cloud Integration and Hybrid Solutions

As businesses increasingly move toward digital transformation, integrating SQL Server with cloud environments has become essential for many organizations. Cloud computing offers significant benefits, including scalability, flexibility, cost-efficiency, and enhanced disaster recovery options. SQL Server, a critical component of many enterprise IT infrastructures, is now well-equipped to integrate with cloud services, providing organizations with powerful hybrid solutions that combine on-premises capabilities with the advantages of the cloud. These cloud and hybrid integration solutions enable SQL Server to scale dynamically, optimize resource utilization, and provide more reliable, accessible, and cost-effective solutions for managing data and applications. This chapter explores the integration of SQL Server with cloud environments, highlighting the benefits, implementation strategies, and best practices for leveraging cloud and hybrid solutions effectively.

SQL Server's integration with cloud environments allows organizations to take advantage of the cloud's flexibility while maintaining the control and security of their on-premises systems. Microsoft Azure, as the primary cloud platform for SQL Server, provides robust services for hosting, managing, and scaling SQL Server instances. Azure offers a variety of cloud-based SQL Server services, such as Azure SQL Database, which provides a fully managed database service, and SQL Server on Azure Virtual Machines (VMs), which allows users to deploy a SQL Server instance on a virtual machine running in the cloud. Azure also provides a variety of hybrid solutions that enable businesses to seamlessly extend their on-premises SQL Server instances to the cloud, creating a unified and flexible environment for managing data.

One of the most common scenarios for SQL Server cloud integration is using Azure SQL Database, which allows organizations to offload the management of SQL Server instances to Microsoft, freeing up IT resources to focus on more strategic tasks. Azure SQL Database is a Platform-as-a-Service (PaaS) offering that provides high availability, automatic backups, patching, and scaling without requiring manual intervention from administrators. It is ideal for workloads that require rapid scaling and high availability but do not require full control over the underlying infrastructure. Organizations that use Azure SQL Database can take advantage of automatic performance tuning, built-in security features, and advanced data analytics capabilities, all while minimizing the administrative burden of managing hardware, backups, and updates.

For organizations that require more control over their SQL Server instances, SQL Server on Azure VMs provides a flexible and scalable solution. This Infrastructure-as-a-Service (IaaS) offering allows businesses to deploy full instances of SQL Server on virtual machines in the Azure cloud. With SQL Server on Azure VMs, organizations can use their existing licensing and configurations, providing a familiar environment for database administrators. The ability to scale up or scale out resources on-demand makes this option suitable for large-scale applications, complex workloads, and high-traffic environments. Additionally, using SQL Server on Azure VMs allows organizations to maintain full control over their SQL Server instances, including configuring custom settings and installing third-party applications.

Hybrid solutions, where organizations integrate on-premises SQL Server with cloud services, are becoming increasingly popular as businesses seek to balance the benefits of the cloud with the need for control over sensitive data. A hybrid SQL Server environment allows businesses to extend their on-premises infrastructure into the cloud, creating a flexible and scalable data environment that can be optimized for different workloads. Azure Hybrid Benefit, for example, allows businesses to use their existing on-premises SQL Server licenses to reduce costs when migrating to the cloud. This benefit can significantly lower the total cost of ownership for organizations that want to adopt cloud solutions without losing their existing investments in SQL Server licenses.

Another important aspect of SQL Server cloud integration is the ability to enable hybrid disaster recovery solutions. Organizations can leverage the cloud as a backup and disaster recovery site for their on-premises SQL Server databases, creating a resilient environment that ensures business continuity in the event of a failure. Azure Site Recovery, for instance, can be used to replicate SQL Server instances running on-premises to the cloud, enabling fast failover in the event of a disaster. Similarly, Azure Backup can be used to perform automated backups of SQL Server databases to the cloud, ensuring that data is protected and can be quickly restored in the event of data loss or corruption.

In addition to disaster recovery, cloud integration also enables organizations to leverage cloud-based data analytics and machine learning capabilities. By integrating SQL Server with Azure services such as Azure Data Factory, Azure Machine Learning, and Azure Synapse Analytics, businesses can unlock new insights from their data. These services allow SQL Server data to be seamlessly transferred to cloud-based analytics tools, where it can be analyzed in real-time or used to build predictive models that drive business intelligence. SQL Server's integration with these Azure services facilitates the creation of powerful data pipelines and the automation of data workflows, streamlining business processes and providing valuable insights that inform decision-making.

Security and compliance are critical considerations when integrating SQL Server with cloud environments. Azure provides robust security features, including data encryption, identity and access management, and threat detection. SQL Server databases hosted in the cloud benefit from these features, ensuring that data is protected both in transit and at rest. Azure Security Center and Azure Active Directory can be used to monitor and manage access to SQL Server instances, while Azure's built-in compliance certifications ensure that organizations can meet industry standards and regulatory requirements. SQL Server's integration with Azure Key Vault also allows for secure storage and management of database credentials, keys, and other sensitive information, ensuring that security policies are consistently enforced across both on-premises and cloud environments.

As organizations continue to move toward cloud and hybrid solutions, optimizing performance and managing costs become increasingly important. Cloud integration allows businesses to scale their SQL Server environments dynamically, ensuring that they can meet fluctuating demands without overcommitting resources. Azure's auto-scaling capabilities enable SQL Server instances to automatically adjust resources based on workload requirements, providing an efficient and cost-effective solution for managing workloads that experience peaks and valleys in usage. Additionally, SQL Server on Azure Virtual Machines can take advantage of Azure's cost management and billing tools to monitor and optimize usage, ensuring that businesses only pay for the resources they need.

Integrating SQL Server with the cloud offers significant advantages for organizations seeking to modernize their IT infrastructure, improve scalability, and optimize data management processes. By using cloud-based solutions such as Azure SQL Database, SQL Server on Azure VMs, and hybrid architectures, businesses can extend their on-premises databases to the cloud and take advantage of cloud-based features such as automated backups, disaster recovery, and data analytics. The ability to seamlessly integrate on-premises SQL Server instances with Azure services allows businesses to leverage the best of both worlds, ensuring that their data is highly available, secure, and optimized for performance. As the adoption of cloud and hybrid solutions continues to grow, organizations must focus on implementing best practices for cloud integration to ensure that they can fully realize the benefits of cloud computing while maintaining control over their SQL Server environments.

# Implementing SQL Server in Virtualized Environments

Virtualization has revolutionized IT infrastructure by allowing organizations to run multiple operating systems and applications on a single physical machine. SQL Server, as a critical component in many organizations' IT environments, benefits greatly from virtualization, providing flexibility, scalability, and improved resource utilization. Implementing SQL Server in virtualized environments, such as VMware, Hyper-V, or other virtualization platforms, offers several advantages, but it also comes with unique challenges that need to be addressed to ensure optimal performance and reliability. This chapter explores the considerations, best practices, and strategies for deploying SQL Server in virtualized environments, highlighting the key factors that impact performance, resource management, and system reliability.

When implementing SQL Server in virtualized environments, the first consideration is ensuring that the underlying virtual infrastructure is properly configured to meet the resource demands of SQL Server. SQL Server is a resource-intensive application, requiring sufficient CPU, memory, and disk resources to perform well. One of the key benefits of virtualization is its ability to allocate resources dynamically, allowing administrators to adjust resource allocation based on workload demands. However, to achieve optimal performance, it is essential to allocate resources carefully and avoid overcommitting physical resources, which can lead to contention and performance degradation. Administrators should monitor CPU, memory, and disk usage regularly to ensure that SQL Server instances are receiving adequate resources and that the virtual machines (VMs) hosting SQL Server are not overburdened by other workloads.

When setting up SQL Server in a virtualized environment, one of the most important considerations is determining whether to deploy SQL Server as a standalone virtual machine or as part of a virtualized cluster. In a standalone VM configuration, SQL Server runs on a single virtual machine, which can be easily scaled by adjusting the allocated CPU, memory, and storage resources. This setup is suitable for smaller environments or non-mission-critical workloads, where high availability and fault tolerance are not as critical. In contrast, implementing SQL Server in a virtualized cluster, such as a Hyper-V or VMware cluster, provides high availability by enabling automatic failover between multiple virtual machines. This setup is ideal for organizations that require fault tolerance and system redundancy, as it ensures that SQL Server instances remain available even in the event of hardware failure.

Another important consideration when deploying SQL Server in virtualized environments is the storage architecture. SQL Server's performance is heavily dependent on disk I/O, and virtualized environments can introduce additional overhead in terms of storage performance. Virtual disks in a virtual machine share the underlying physical storage resources with other VMs, which can result in I/O contention, especially in environments with high database workloads. To mitigate this risk, it is recommended to use high-performance storage solutions, such as solid-state drives (SSDs), and to configure storage with sufficient throughput to handle SQL Server's I/O demands. Additionally, it is important to avoid placing SQL Server data, transaction logs, and tempdb on the same virtual disk, as this can lead to contention and performance degradation. Separating these files onto different virtual disks or physical storage devices is a best practice to ensure that each component of SQL Server has access to the required I/O resources.

Memory management is another key consideration when running SQL Server in a virtualized environment. SQL Server is designed to take advantage of large amounts of memory to improve query performance by caching data and execution plans. Virtualization platforms, however, allocate memory to virtual machines dynamically, which can lead to issues such as memory overcommitment, where the total allocated memory for all VMs exceeds the physical memory available on the host machine. This can cause paging, which negatively impacts performance. To avoid memory overcommitment, it is essential to carefully allocate memory to SQL Server instances based on their workload requirements and to monitor memory usage regularly. Virtualization platforms such as VMware and Hyper-V offer memory ballooning and memory swapping mechanisms that can be used to manage memory allocation dynamically, but these features should be used cautiously to avoid performance issues with SQL Server.

CPU allocation is another critical factor that can affect SQL Server's performance in a virtualized environment. SQL Server is a multi-threaded application, and its performance can be significantly impacted by CPU contention, particularly in environments with many VMs running on the same host. Virtualization platforms allow administrators to allocate multiple virtual CPUs (vCPUs) to a virtual machine, but allocating too many vCPUs can lead to inefficient CPU scheduling and increased overhead. It is essential to allocate the appropriate number of vCPUs based on SQL Server's workload and to ensure that the underlying physical CPUs are not overcommitted. SQL Server instances should also be configured with an appropriate maximum degree of parallelism (MaxDOP) to ensure efficient CPU usage, particularly in multi-core environments.

Networking is another area where virtualization can introduce complexities. SQL Server relies on fast, reliable network connections for communication between instances, clients, and other services. In a virtualized environment, network performance can be affected by factors such as network virtualization, network congestion, and shared resources. To optimize networking performance, it is important to use high-speed network interfaces and configure the virtualized network infrastructure to minimize latency and maximize throughput. Additionally, network interfaces for SQL Server instances should be isolated from other virtual machines to avoid competition for network resources.

One of the major advantages of implementing SQL Server in virtualized environments is the ability to implement efficient backup and disaster recovery strategies. Virtualization platforms provide tools for snapshotting and cloning virtual machines, which can be used to create backups of SQL Server instances quickly and efficiently. While virtual machine snapshots are useful for creating backups, they should be used with caution when dealing with SQL Server, as they can introduce issues with transactional consistency. It is recommended to use SQL Server's built-in backup tools, such as full, differential, and transaction log backups, in combination with the virtualization platform's backup tools to ensure data consistency and minimize the risk of data corruption. Additionally, integrating SQL Server with cloud-based disaster recovery solutions or storage systems can provide further protection against hardware failures and data loss.

High availability and failover clustering are crucial for maintaining uptime in virtualized environments. SQL Server can be configured for high availability using features such as AlwaysOn Availability Groups, failover clustering, and database mirroring, which can all be implemented in virtualized environments. For example, SQL Server failover clustering can be used with Hyper-V or VMware to create a virtualized cluster that provides automatic failover in the event of a failure. The virtualized environment can also be used to replicate SQL Server instances to remote locations, providing additional redundancy and protection against site-wide failures. By combining these high availability solutions with the flexibility and scalability of virtualization, organizations can ensure that their SQL Server environments remain resilient and available even in the face of hardware or software failures.

Finally, performance monitoring and optimization are essential when running SQL Server in virtualized environments. Virtualization introduces an additional layer of abstraction, which can make it more difficult to diagnose and resolve performance issues. To effectively monitor SQL Server's performance, administrators should use both SQL Server's built-in monitoring tools, such as Dynamic Management Views (DMVs) and SQL Server Profiler, as well as virtualization-specific monitoring tools that provide insights into resource usage at the hypervisor level. These tools can help identify resource contention, such as CPU, memory, or disk bottlenecks, and enable administrators to optimize resource allocation to ensure that SQL Server performs at its best in a virtualized environment.

Implementing SQL Server in virtualized environments offers significant benefits, including flexibility, scalability, and cost efficiency. However, it also requires careful planning and attention to resource allocation, storage configuration, and network performance to ensure optimal performance and reliability. By following best practices for memory management, CPU allocation, storage configuration, and backup strategies, administrators can maximize the benefits of SQL Server in virtualized environments while minimizing potential risks and performance challenges.

# SQL Server Licensing and Cost Management

SQL Server licensing can be complex, with a range of options available depending on the edition, the type of deployment, and the specific use case. Choosing the right licensing model is crucial for organizations seeking to optimize costs while ensuring that they comply with licensing requirements. Microsoft offers multiple SQL Server licensing models, each designed to cater to different types of users and use cases, from small businesses to large enterprises. These licensing options include per-core licensing, Server + CAL (Client Access License) licensing, and subscription-based models, among others. Managing these licenses effectively requires a deep understanding of the various models, their implications for cost, and how to monitor and track usage to avoid over-licensing or under-licensing, which could result in compliance issues or unnecessary expenses.

The per-core licensing model is the most commonly used for modern SQL Server deployments, particularly in environments with high resource demands. Under this model, organizations purchase licenses based on the number of physical or virtual cores on the server that will be running SQL Server. This model is designed to scale with the performance of the hardware and is most appropriate for larger environments or cloud-based implementations where scalability and flexibility are paramount. It offers a straightforward way to license high-performance servers, but it can become expensive if a large number of cores are involved, as each core requires a separate license. Additionally, organizations may need to consider how they manage licensing in virtualized environments, where multiple virtual machines (VMs) may be running SQL Server instances on shared physical hardware.

For those with less demanding environments or smaller deployments, the Server + CAL licensing model can be more cost-effective. This model involves purchasing a license for each server running SQL Server, as well as a separate license for each user or device that will access the server. The Server + CAL model is ideal for organizations with a smaller number of users or devices that need access to SQL Server and do not require the scalability offered by the per-core model. However, the CAL licensing approach becomes less practical in large-scale environments or cloud environments where the number of users or devices is rapidly increasing. While it may offer lower upfront costs compared to per-core licensing, organizations need to ensure that they track the number of CALs accurately to avoid compliance issues.

In recent years, Microsoft has introduced subscription-based models for SQL Server licensing, particularly in cloud environments. These models are generally more flexible than traditional perpetual licenses and are ideal for organizations that need to scale rapidly or adopt a pay-as-you-go approach. Subscription-based licenses are typically offered through cloud providers such as Microsoft Azure, where SQL Server is available as part of the cloud infrastructure services. With this model, organizations pay for SQL Server on a monthly or annual basis, based on the usage and resources consumed. This approach can be highly cost-effective for organizations with variable workloads or short-term projects, as it eliminates the need for large upfront investments. However, it's important to monitor usage carefully, as overuse can result in higher costs than expected. Subscription-based models are often easier to scale, as organizations can adjust their licensing as their needs change.

Beyond the primary licensing models, organizations must also consider additional costs related to licensing for features such as high availability, business intelligence, and data warehousing. SQL Server offers several editions, such as the Standard, Enterprise, and Web editions, each with different feature sets. The Enterprise edition includes advanced features like AlwaysOn Availability Groups, partitioned tables, and advanced analytics, which are ideal for large-scale applications and mission-critical workloads. However, the Enterprise edition comes with a higher price tag compared to the Standard edition, and organizations must carefully assess whether they need the advanced features or if a lower-tier edition would suffice for their use case. For many organizations, especially those with limited budgets, the Standard edition provides an adequate feature set at a lower cost.

Another important factor to consider when managing SQL Server licenses is ensuring compliance with Microsoft's licensing policies. Microsoft conducts audits to ensure that organizations are using their software in accordance with the terms of their licenses. An audit can result in penalties or additional costs if an organization is found to be under-licensed or using SQL Server in ways that violate the terms of the license agreement. To avoid such issues, organizations should establish a rigorous process for tracking and managing SQL Server licenses, including maintaining accurate records of purchases, deployments, and usage. Licensing audits can be complex, particularly in large or cloud-based environments, where instances of SQL Server may be spread across multiple physical and virtual machines. To ensure compliance, organizations should use tools such as Microsoft's License Mobility or Software Asset Management (SAM) tools, which help track license usage and ensure that they remain compliant with licensing agreements.

Cost management is also a critical aspect of SQL Server licensing, particularly for organizations that are operating on tight budgets. SQL Server can become expensive, especially in large-scale environments or when running high-availability solutions like failover clusters and AlwaysOn Availability Groups. Organizations need to regularly assess their licensing needs and usage to ensure they are not over-spending on licenses they don't need. For example, organizations can optimize costs by using reserved instances in cloud environments, where they commit to a set usage level over a specified period in exchange for lower pricing. Similarly, in on-premises deployments, organizations can optimize licensing by consolidating workloads or using virtualization technologies to ensure that SQL Server instances are running on properly licensed virtual machines with the right allocation of resources.

Furthermore, managing the cost of SQL Server licenses extends beyond the initial purchase to include ongoing expenses such as software updates, support, and maintenance. Microsoft offers Software Assurance (SA) as an optional add-on for SQL Server licenses, which provides access to software updates, new versions, and support services. While Software Assurance can provide significant value by ensuring access to the latest features and security updates, it comes at an additional cost. Organizations must evaluate whether the benefits of Software Assurance outweigh the costs based on their specific needs and usage patterns. In some cases, it may make sense to opt for the base license and handle updates and support on an as-needed basis, particularly for organizations with limited budgets or predictable workloads.

Effective SQL Server licensing and cost management requires a strategic approach that balances the organization's need for performance and scalability with its budgetary constraints. By understanding the various licensing models and editions, tracking usage accurately, and optimizing license allocation, organizations can ensure that they are using SQL Server efficiently and within their budget. With the right licensing strategy in place, businesses can unlock the full potential of SQL Server while avoiding unnecessary costs and maintaining compliance with Microsoft's licensing policies.

# Best Practices for SQL Server Deployment

Deploying SQL Server in an enterprise environment requires careful planning, configuration, and implementation to ensure high availability, performance, scalability, and security. A successful deployment goes beyond the basic installation of SQL Server; it involves making strategic decisions regarding hardware, networking, configuration settings, security policies, backup strategies, and ongoing maintenance. Adhering to best practices during the deployment process not only optimizes performance but also sets the foundation for a stable and reliable SQL Server environment. This chapter discusses key best practices for SQL Server deployment, focusing on aspects such as system configuration, hardware considerations, network setup, security measures, and backup strategies.

One of the first steps in SQL Server deployment is choosing the appropriate hardware to meet the system's performance requirements.

SQL Server is a resource-intensive application, so it is essential to select hardware that can handle the anticipated workload. When selecting hardware, it is crucial to consider factors such as CPU, memory, and storage. SQL Server performs best with high-performance processors, ample RAM, and fast storage systems, particularly when dealing with large databases or complex queries. A multi-core processor with high clock speeds is typically recommended, as SQL Server is a multi-threaded application that benefits from parallel processing. Memory is also a critical factor; SQL Server uses memory for caching data, query plans, and other processes, so having enough RAM can significantly improve query performance. For storage, it is best to use fast disks, such as solid-state drives (SSDs), to reduce I/O latency and improve read/write speeds, especially for the SQL Server data files and transaction logs.

Proper configuration of SQL Server is another essential aspect of deployment. One important step in configuration is ensuring that SQL Server is installed with the right edition. Microsoft offers several editions of SQL Server, including Enterprise, Standard, and Web, each tailored for different use cases and organizational sizes. The Enterprise edition offers the most advanced features, such as high availability, advanced analytics, and scalability, while the Standard edition is more cost-effective and suitable for smaller environments. It is important to assess the needs of the organization to determine the most appropriate edition, considering factors such as the size of the database, the required features, and the available budget.

SQL Server installation and configuration also involve selecting the appropriate collation settings, which determine how SQL Server handles character data and sorts text. Choosing the correct collation is critical for ensuring that SQL Server correctly processes data, especially when dealing with multilingual databases or systems that integrate with other applications. Additionally, administrators should configure the SQL Server instance with appropriate settings for memory allocation, parallel processing, and other performance-related parameters. It is recommended to configure SQL Server to use a fixed amount of memory rather than allowing it to use all available system memory, as this can lead to memory contention issues. Additionally, SQL Server's Maximum Degree of Parallelism (MaxDOP) setting should be configured based on the number of CPU cores and the nature of the workload to ensure that queries are executed efficiently.

Network configuration plays a vital role in SQL Server performance and deployment. A high-speed network connection is essential to ensure that SQL Server can efficiently handle communication between clients, applications, and other services. In many environments, SQL Server instances need to be accessible across multiple networks, whether for remote access or distributed applications. It is essential to configure the network properly, including setting up the appropriate IP addresses, TCP/IP protocols, and port configurations to ensure reliable and secure communication. SQL Server also supports network encryption, which can be configured to protect sensitive data during transmission. For high-availability deployments, configuring network settings to support failover clustering or AlwaysOn Availability Groups is critical to ensure seamless failover in the event of server or network failures.

Security is one of the most important considerations when deploying SQL Server, as the database stores sensitive organizational data that could be targeted by cyberattacks. Implementing strong security measures from the outset is critical for protecting the integrity and confidentiality of the data. The principle of least privilege should be applied to SQL Server accounts, ensuring that users and applications only have access to the data and functionality that they absolutely need. Administrators should configure SQL Server authentication carefully, choosing between Windows authentication and mixed-mode authentication based on the organization's security policies. Windows authentication is generally more secure, as it integrates with Active Directory, providing centralized control over access. SQL Server also supports transparent data encryption (TDE), which encrypts database files to protect data at rest. Additionally, configuring SQL Server's built-in auditing features can help monitor and log access to sensitive data, ensuring that unauthorized access attempts are detected and addressed promptly.

Another critical security measure is configuring firewalls to control access to SQL Server instances. SQL Server should be deployed behind a properly configured firewall, and only trusted IP addresses should be allowed to access the database server. Using VPNs or other secure tunneling technologies can provide an additional layer of security for remote access to SQL Server. Securing SQL Server with SSL certificates for encrypted communication between clients and servers is also a best practice for protecting sensitive data from being intercepted during transmission.

In addition to security, backup strategies must be part of the deployment plan. SQL Server databases should be backed up regularly to ensure data protection in case of hardware failures, corruption, or accidental deletion. The backup strategy should include full, differential, and transaction log backups to ensure that data can be restored to a specific point in time, minimizing data loss. Administrators should configure SQL Server to back up databases to offsite locations or cloud storage to protect against data loss in case of physical disasters, such as fire or flooding. It is also essential to perform periodic restore tests to ensure that backups are functional and that the restoration process is efficient and reliable. Integrating SQL Server backup processes with automated monitoring tools can help ensure that backups are performed regularly and any failures are quickly addressed.

For high availability and disaster recovery, deploying SQL Server in a high-availability configuration such as AlwaysOn Availability Groups or SQL Server failover clustering can help ensure that the database remains operational even in the event of hardware or software failures. AlwaysOn Availability Groups provide automatic failover capabilities, allowing SQL Server to switch to a secondary replica when the primary instance fails. This setup can also allow for read-write operations on the primary replica while offloading read-only queries to secondary replicas, improving overall system performance. SQL Server failover clustering provides an additional layer of redundancy by allowing multiple SQL Server instances to work together as a single cluster, with automatic failover in case of a server failure.

Monitoring is another vital aspect of SQL Server deployment. Administrators should configure SQL Server to send alerts for performance issues, such as high CPU usage, memory pressure, or disk space issues. Using SQL Server Management Studio (SSMS) or third-party monitoring tools, administrators can track important performance metrics and proactively address issues before they impact end users. Monitoring tools can also help identify long-running queries, blocking issues, and other performance bottlenecks, enabling administrators to take corrective actions quickly. Regular performance assessments should be performed to ensure that SQL Server is optimized and running efficiently.

SQL Server deployment requires a multi-faceted approach, combining hardware, software, security, and performance management to ensure that the database environment is reliable, secure, and scalable. By following best practices in these areas, organizations can ensure that their SQL Server instances are set up for optimal performance, high availability, and long-term success. Through careful planning, configuration, and monitoring, businesses can build a robust SQL Server environment that supports their data management needs and scales with their growth.

# Troubleshooting SQL Server Errors and Issues

SQL Server is a powerful and robust database management system, but like any complex software, it is susceptible to errors and issues that can disrupt its performance, availability, and security. Troubleshooting SQL Server errors and issues requires a systematic approach that combines knowledge of SQL Server internals, effective diagnostic tools, and a clear understanding of the error messages and their implications. Errors in SQL Server can arise from a variety of causes, such as hardware failures, network issues, configuration problems, or corrupt data. The ability to quickly identify and resolve these issues is critical for minimizing downtime and ensuring that the system remains operational. This chapter explores common SQL Server errors and issues, the tools available for diagnosing and resolving them, and best practices for effective troubleshooting.

When SQL Server encounters an error, it often generates an error message that provides valuable information about the cause of the issue. Error messages in SQL Server are typically displayed in the SQL Server Management Studio (SSMS) or in the SQL Server error log.

These messages may include an error code, a description of the problem, and additional details that can help pinpoint the root cause of the issue. Understanding these error messages is the first step in troubleshooting SQL Server problems. SQL Server error codes follow a specific format, often consisting of a number followed by a description. For example, error code 18456 indicates a login failure, while error code 9002 signals that the transaction log is full. SQL Server's error messages also provide severity levels, which indicate the seriousness of the problem. Errors with a severity level of 16 or higher are typically considered critical and require immediate attention.

One common issue in SQL Server is performance degradation due to resource contention, such as high CPU usage, excessive memory consumption, or disk I/O bottlenecks. High CPU usage can be caused by inefficient queries, poorly optimized indexes, or an insufficient number of CPU resources assigned to SQL Server. To diagnose high CPU usage, administrators can use SQL Server's built-in Dynamic Management Views (DMVs) to query performance data and identify the queries or processes consuming the most CPU time. The sys.dm_exec_requests DMV provides information on currently executing queries, while sys.dm_exec_query_stats helps identify long-running queries. By analyzing these views, administrators can optimize queries, create appropriate indexes, or adjust SQL Server's resource allocation to alleviate the CPU strain.

Memory issues are another common cause of SQL Server errors, especially in systems with large databases or heavy workloads. SQL Server relies heavily on memory for caching data and query plans, and inadequate memory allocation can lead to performance issues or even system crashes. SQL Server provides several tools for diagnosing memory issues, including the sys.dm_os_memory_clerks DMV, which provides details on how memory is being used by SQL Server components. Administrators can monitor memory pressure by reviewing SQL Server's memory usage in conjunction with system-level memory metrics, such as those provided by Windows Performance Monitor. If memory issues are detected, solutions may include adjusting SQL Server's memory settings, adding physical memory to the system, or optimizing queries to reduce memory consumption.

Disk I/O problems can also significantly impact SQL Server performance. SQL Server's reliance on disk storage for data, transaction logs, and tempdb means that slow disk performance or insufficient disk space can lead to database slowdowns, timeouts, and errors. To diagnose disk I/O issues, administrators can use the sys.dm_io_virtual_file_stats DMV, which provides information on the read and write performance of database files. Additionally, administrators should monitor disk usage regularly to ensure that there is enough space for transaction logs and database files. If disk I/O bottlenecks are identified, solutions may include moving database files to faster storage, optimizing indexes to reduce disk reads, or increasing the size of disk volumes to prevent space issues.

Another common issue in SQL Server is deadlocks, which occur when two or more transactions are blocked, each waiting for the other to release resources. Deadlocks can severely impact system performance and result in errors if not addressed promptly. SQL Server automatically detects deadlocks and terminates one of the transactions involved, rolling back the affected transaction to resolve the deadlock. To diagnose deadlocks, administrators can use SQL Server Profiler to capture deadlock graphs, which provide a visual representation of the transactions and resources involved in the deadlock. Once a deadlock is identified, administrators can analyze the graph to determine the root cause, which may involve optimizing queries, adjusting transaction isolation levels, or modifying the database schema to reduce resource contention.

Corruption of database files or transaction logs can also lead to SQL Server errors. Data corruption can occur for various reasons, including hardware failures, improper shutdowns, or software bugs. SQL Server provides several tools for detecting and addressing corruption, with the DBCC CHECKDB command being the most commonly used tool for checking database integrity. This command scans the database for physical and logical corruption and provides recommendations for repairing any detected issues. If corruption is detected, administrators should restore the affected database from a known good backup or use the DBCC CHECKDB repair options if no backup is available. It is important to regularly run integrity checks to catch corruption early before it results in data loss or system instability.

SQL Server login issues are another common source of errors. Errors such as "Login failed for user" (error 18456) typically indicate that the user credentials are incorrect or that the user does not have the necessary permissions to access the database. To troubleshoot login issues, administrators should review the SQL Server error log, which provides detailed information about failed login attempts, including the error state that indicates the specific cause of the failure. Common causes of login issues include incorrect login credentials, missing login accounts, or insufficient permissions granted to the user. To resolve these issues, administrators can ensure that the correct logins are created, verify that users are assigned the appropriate roles, and check the SQL Server authentication mode to ensure that it is configured correctly.

SQL Server replication issues can also cause errors, particularly in environments that use transactional or merge replication. Replication problems can occur due to network failures, conflicts between replicated data, or issues with the replication agents. To diagnose replication issues, administrators should use the sp_replmonitorhelpsubscription stored procedure to view the status of replication subscriptions and identify any synchronization problems. Additionally, the replication monitor tool in SQL Server Management Studio provides a comprehensive view of the replication topology and allows administrators to track the health of replication processes. Resolving replication issues often involves troubleshooting network connectivity, resolving data conflicts, or reinitializing replication subscriptions.

To troubleshoot SQL Server errors effectively, administrators must adopt a structured approach that includes gathering relevant diagnostic information, analyzing error logs, and leveraging the right tools and DMVs. SQL Server provides a wealth of diagnostic features, such as extended events, SQL Server Profiler, and system views, that can help pinpoint the root cause of issues. Regularly reviewing error logs, monitoring performance, and conducting proactive maintenance can help prevent many common issues before they affect end-users. By implementing a robust troubleshooting process and staying proactive with monitoring, SQL Server administrators can ensure that their environments remain stable, efficient, and reliable, minimizing the impact of errors and improving overall database health.

# Automating SQL Server Backups and Restores

Automating SQL Server backups and restores is a critical aspect of database administration that ensures data integrity, minimizes downtime, and enhances disaster recovery capabilities. Backups are essential for protecting data from corruption, hardware failures, human errors, and other unforeseen events that can lead to data loss. SQL Server provides a variety of backup types, including full, differential, and transaction log backups, each serving a unique purpose in maintaining the safety and availability of the database. By automating the backup and restore processes, administrators can ensure that backups are performed consistently, on schedule, and with minimal intervention, ultimately reducing the risk of human error and improving recovery time objectives (RTO) and recovery point objectives (RPO).

SQL Server provides several tools and methods to automate backups, including SQL Server Management Studio (SSMS), SQL Server Agent, and PowerShell scripts. One of the most commonly used tools for automation is SQL Server Agent, a built-in component of SQL Server that allows administrators to schedule and automate jobs, including backup tasks. By configuring SQL Server Agent to run backup jobs on a regular schedule, administrators can ensure that backups are performed without manual intervention. SQL Server Agent allows for the creation of custom jobs, each consisting of one or more steps, which can include running a T-SQL script or executing a specific backup command. These jobs can be scheduled to run at predefined intervals, such as daily, weekly, or monthly, depending on the organization's backup strategy.

In SQL Server Agent, administrators can configure full backups, differential backups, and transaction log backups to be executed on a set schedule. Full backups capture the entire database, including all data and objects, while differential backups only capture the changes made since the last full backup. Transaction log backups, on the other hand, capture all transactions that have occurred since the last log backup, enabling point-in-time recovery. Automating these backups ensures that organizations maintain a comprehensive and up-to-date backup set, allowing for fast and reliable restores in the event of data loss.

When setting up automated backups, it is important to consider the retention policy for backup files. Backup files consume storage space, and without a proper retention strategy, organizations may find themselves running out of storage or maintaining outdated backups. SQL Server provides several ways to manage backup retention, including the use of backup expiration dates, which allow administrators to specify how long backups should be retained before they are deleted. Additionally, administrators can configure SQL Server Agent to automatically delete old backups after they reach a certain age or size, helping to free up space and keep the backup environment organized.

To ensure that backups are performed successfully and that any issues are quickly identified, administrators should configure alerts in SQL Server Agent. Alerts can be set up to notify administrators when a backup job fails, when the backup completes successfully, or when a specific threshold is met (e.g., disk space usage or backup duration). These alerts can be sent via email, Windows Event Logs, or other notification channels, allowing administrators to take immediate action if a backup job encounters a problem. Monitoring and alerting are essential for maintaining the reliability of automated backup processes, as they help identify issues before they escalate and ensure that backups are completed as expected.

Another key tool for automating SQL Server backups is PowerShell, which provides a scripting environment for administrators to automate backup tasks. PowerShell scripts can be used to create custom backup routines that are more flexible than SQL Server Agent jobs, allowing for advanced configurations such as conditional backups based on server load or database size. PowerShell also allows for easy integration with other automation platforms, such as Microsoft System Center or third-party backup solutions, providing a centralized approach to backup management. Administrators can use PowerShell to automate full, differential, and transaction log backups, as well as to perform tasks like compressing backup files, encrypting backups, or uploading them to remote storage locations.

In addition to automating backups, it is equally important to automate the restore process. While backups are essential for data protection, the ability to restore data quickly and efficiently is just as critical, especially in the event of a disaster or system failure. Automating the restore process helps ensure that organizations can meet their recovery objectives, minimize downtime, and reduce human intervention during the recovery process. SQL Server provides several ways to automate restores, including the use of SQL Server Agent and PowerShell scripts.

SQL Server Agent can be used to automate restore operations, particularly in scenarios where databases need to be restored from backup as part of a regular maintenance routine, such as in test or development environments. For example, administrators can create a SQL Server Agent job that automatically restores a database from the most recent full backup, followed by the application of the appropriate differential or transaction log backups. This process can be scheduled to occur during off-peak hours, ensuring that the restore operation does not interfere with production workloads.

PowerShell can also be used to automate database restores, particularly in more complex or customized scenarios. PowerShell scripts can be written to perform point-in-time restores by applying transaction log backups in sequence, or to restore a specific backup based on criteria such as the backup file date or the database name. Additionally, PowerShell can be used to integrate SQL Server restore operations with other systems, such as monitoring and alerting platforms, to ensure that restores are tracked and any issues are reported in real time.

While automating the backup and restore process can significantly reduce administrative overhead, it is also important to regularly test the backups and the restore process to ensure that they are reliable. Backup testing involves restoring backups to a separate system or environment and verifying that the data is intact, consistent, and usable. This testing should be performed periodically to ensure that backups can be restored successfully in the event of a disaster. Automating the testing process, where possible, helps ensure that backup verification is part of the regular maintenance routine and that issues are detected early.

Additionally, automating SQL Server backups and restores can be further enhanced by integrating with cloud storage solutions. Cloud-based backups offer an offsite solution for storing backup files, providing added protection against disasters that may affect on-premises infrastructure. SQL Server can be configured to automatically back up databases to cloud storage providers, such as Microsoft Azure Blob Storage or Amazon S3, using custom scripts or third-party tools. Cloud backups can be automated using SQL Server Agent jobs, PowerShell scripts, or backup solutions that support cloud integration, ensuring that backup files are securely stored offsite and can be easily restored if necessary.

Automating SQL Server backups and restores is a critical practice for ensuring the protection and availability of data in SQL Server environments. By leveraging tools such as SQL Server Agent, PowerShell, and cloud storage, organizations can reduce the risk of data loss, minimize downtime, and streamline backup and recovery operations. Regular monitoring, alerting, and testing are essential components of an automated backup and restore strategy, helping administrators maintain the reliability and efficiency of their backup processes. With the right automation in place, organizations can confidently protect their data and ensure that they can quickly recover from any disruptions.

# SQL Server Data Migration Strategies

Data migration is a crucial aspect of managing SQL Server environments, particularly in situations where organizations need to upgrade their systems, move to new hardware, or transition to cloud-based infrastructure. Migrating data effectively requires careful planning, coordination, and execution to ensure that data is transferred without loss or corruption, while minimizing downtime and ensuring that the new environment performs efficiently. SQL Server offers a range of tools and strategies for data migration, each suited to different types of migration scenarios. These strategies must take into account factors such as data size, complexity, destination environment, and the level of downtime the organization is willing to tolerate. The goal of a successful data migration strategy is not only to move data but also to optimize it for the new system while maintaining its integrity and performance.

The first step in any SQL Server data migration process is assessing the environment and defining the migration objectives. This includes identifying the source SQL Server instance, understanding the structure of the data, determining the target environment, and evaluating any potential challenges or requirements. A key consideration during this phase is whether the migration involves an upgrade to a new version of SQL Server, a move to a different type of SQL Server instance (such as migrating from on-premises to SQL Server on Azure), or a shift to a completely new platform altogether. The migration strategy will differ significantly depending on whether it is an in-place upgrade, a cross-platform migration, or a cloud migration.

For SQL Server migration projects that involve upgrading to a newer version of SQL Server, the first priority is ensuring compatibility between the source and target versions. Microsoft provides a variety of tools, such as the SQL Server Data Migration Assistant (DMA), which helps assess database compatibility, identifies potential issues, and provides recommendations for resolving them. The DMA is particularly useful for assessing deprecated features, breaking changes, and performance issues that could arise when moving to a newer version of SQL Server. Ensuring that applications, stored procedures, and other SQL Server features are compatible with the target version is a critical part of the planning process. Administrators should test the migrated data in a non-production environment to validate its integrity and performance before the migration is finalized.

For migrations involving cloud environments, such as moving SQL Server databases to Azure SQL Database or SQL Server on Azure Virtual Machines, the process becomes more complex due to the need to manage hybrid environments. Cloud migration often requires additional steps, such as configuring secure network connections, addressing performance concerns associated with latency and bandwidth, and handling issues related to data sovereignty. In these cases, using tools like Azure Database Migration Service (DMS) is essential for ensuring that the data is migrated efficiently and securely. DMS allows for a seamless, automated migration of data from on-premises SQL Server instances to Azure-based solutions, minimizing the need for manual intervention and reducing the risk of errors during the transfer.

When migrating large volumes of data, especially in environments with minimal downtime constraints, it is important to select the right method to minimize disruption to the business. SQL Server offers several techniques for performing data migrations with minimal downtime, such as the backup and restore method, the detach and attach method, and transactional replication. The backup and restore method involves creating a backup of the source database, restoring it in the target environment, and then synchronizing the data to ensure that the migration is completed without data loss. This method works well for relatively simple migrations but may not be suitable for larger, more complex environments where downtime needs to be minimized.

For larger databases or those with more stringent downtime requirements, the detach and attach method is often preferred. This method involves detaching the database from the source SQL Server, moving the database files to the target server, and then attaching them to the target SQL Server instance. This method is faster than a full backup and restore operation and is particularly useful when migrating databases between servers with similar configurations. However, the database must be offline during the process, which can be a limitation in systems that require high availability.

Transactional replication is another powerful strategy for minimizing downtime during data migration. In this approach, data changes are replicated in near real-time from the source SQL Server to the target environment, allowing for continuous synchronization of data during the migration process. Once the replication is complete, a final cutover is performed, and the application is directed to the new environment with minimal downtime. This method is especially useful for scenarios where the source and target environments need to be kept in sync for a prolonged period during the migration.

One of the key challenges in data migration is ensuring that data integrity is maintained throughout the process. Data corruption, inconsistencies, or loss can have significant repercussions for an organization, so it is essential to implement thorough testing and validation processes. Before migrating data, administrators should perform a detailed audit of the source data to identify any anomalies, inconsistencies, or missing records. After the migration, data should be verified using checksums or hash totals to ensure that it matches the source data. Performance tests should also be conducted to ensure that the migrated database performs optimally in the new environment and that any database optimizations or adjustments required for the new platform are implemented.

Another consideration when planning for SQL Server data migration is the impact on business continuity. Many organizations rely on their SQL Server databases for mission-critical applications, and minimizing the impact of the migration on users is essential. It is important to coordinate the migration process with key stakeholders, such as application owners and end-users, to ensure that they are aware of the migration schedule and any potential downtime. During the migration, organizations should also have contingency plans in place to handle unexpected issues or delays that may arise.

Security is another critical aspect of SQL Server data migration. During the migration process, sensitive data must be protected, especially when it is transferred over networks or into cloud environments. Encryption should be used for data in transit to prevent unauthorized access or data breaches. SQL Server provides several built-in features for encrypting data, including Transparent Data Encryption (TDE) and encryption of backups. Organizations should also ensure that security permissions and roles are properly configured in the target environment to prevent unauthorized access to sensitive data after the migration is complete.

Finally, it is essential to implement a comprehensive post-migration strategy to monitor and optimize the SQL Server environment after the migration is complete. This includes monitoring performance metrics, checking for any issues related to database access or functionality, and ensuring that backup and disaster recovery plans are up to date. Any performance or stability issues should be addressed quickly, and database maintenance routines should be adjusted as needed to optimize the system for the new environment. Additionally, post-migration validation should include verifying that all data was successfully migrated and that no data was lost or corrupted during the process.

SQL Server data migration strategies are essential for ensuring that data is moved efficiently, securely, and without disruption. Whether migrating to a new version of SQL Server, moving to the cloud, or transitioning to a different hardware platform, the right strategy can help mitigate risks, reduce downtime, and ensure that business operations continue smoothly. With careful planning, appropriate tools, and a well-structured migration process, organizations can successfully execute SQL Server migrations that meet their performance, security, and business continuity requirements.

# SQL Server Integration with PowerShell

PowerShell is a powerful scripting language and automation framework developed by Microsoft that allows administrators to automate a wide range of tasks across different Microsoft products, including SQL Server. SQL Server integration with PowerShell enables database administrators (DBAs) to manage, configure, and automate various aspects of SQL Server environments, such as database management, backups, monitoring, security, and performance tuning. By leveraging PowerShell scripts, DBAs can streamline operations, improve consistency, and reduce the risk of human error. This chapter explores how SQL Server integrates with PowerShell, including the tools and cmdlets available, the types of tasks that can be automated, and best practices for using PowerShell to manage SQL Server environments effectively.

PowerShell provides a comprehensive set of cmdlets for SQL Server administration through the SQL Server module, which is included with the SQL Server Management Studio (SSMS) installation. The SQL Server module for PowerShell contains several cmdlets designed specifically for interacting with SQL Server instances and databases. These cmdlets enable DBAs to automate routine tasks such as querying databases, managing security, running SQL scripts, and monitoring server health. Some of the most commonly used cmdlets include Invoke-Sqlcmd, Get-SqlInstance, New-SqlDatabase, and Backup-SqlDatabase, among many others.

One of the most common tasks that can be automated with PowerShell is database backup and restore. SQL Server backups are essential for protecting data, and PowerShell scripts can be used to automate backup jobs, set retention policies, and ensure that backups are completed successfully. The Backup-SqlDatabase cmdlet allows DBAs to create full, differential, or transaction log backups directly from PowerShell, providing the flexibility to integrate backups into automated workflows. For instance, administrators can create a PowerShell script that schedules daily backups for multiple databases across several instances, checks the status of the backups, and sends notifications if any backups fail. This automation ensures that backup tasks are performed regularly and that the organization's data is protected without requiring manual intervention.

In addition to backups, SQL Server integration with PowerShell allows administrators to automate the restoration process. Using the Restore-SqlDatabase cmdlet, DBAs can automate database restores in disaster recovery scenarios or for refreshing development and test environments. By scripting the restore process, administrators can quickly recover databases, apply transaction log backups for point-in-time recovery, and manage restore jobs without needing to interact with the SQL Server Management Studio interface. This automation can also be used to ensure that regular restore tests are conducted as part of a disaster recovery plan, confirming that backups are valid and recoverable when needed.

PowerShell also provides tools for managing and monitoring SQL Server performance. The Get-SqlPerformance cmdlet allows administrators to retrieve performance data from SQL Server instances, such as CPU usage, memory usage, disk I/O, and query execution statistics. This data can be used to identify performance bottlenecks, detect potential issues, and monitor the health of the SQL Server environment. Administrators can use PowerShell to create custom performance monitoring scripts that query SQL Server instances at regular intervals, log performance metrics, and trigger alerts if certain thresholds are exceeded. For example, if CPU usage exceeds a specified limit, a PowerShell script can send an email alert to the DBA team, enabling them to take action before performance degradation affects end-users.

Security management is another area where SQL Server and PowerShell integration proves to be valuable. PowerShell scripts can be used to automate user account management, including creating new logins, assigning roles, and auditing access to SQL Server. The New-SqlLogin cmdlet allows DBAs to create logins with specified authentication modes and permissions, while the Set-SqlLogin cmdlet can be used to modify login properties. PowerShell can also automate the process of managing server and database roles, granting or revoking permissions as needed. For instance, a PowerShell script can be used to automatically add or remove users from specific roles based on predefined rules, ensuring that access controls are consistently applied across the organization.

In addition to basic security management, PowerShell can also be used to automate auditing and compliance tasks. SQL Server provides auditing features that can be integrated with PowerShell to track login activity, changes to database objects, and other critical actions. By using PowerShell to query audit logs, administrators can generate compliance reports, review access logs, and identify any unauthorized actions. This capability is particularly important in environments with stringent regulatory requirements, such as healthcare or financial institutions, where detailed tracking of user activity is essential for meeting industry standards.

PowerShell can also be used to automate the deployment and configuration of SQL Server instances. For example, the Install-SqlInstance cmdlet allows DBAs to automate the installation of SQL Server instances on new servers, reducing the time and effort required to set up new environments. Similarly, configuration tasks such as setting the maximum memory limit, configuring server properties, and enabling features like SQL Server Agent or Full-Text Search can all be automated through PowerShell scripts. Automating the deployment and configuration of SQL Server ensures that all instances are set up consistently, reducing the risk of misconfigurations and improving overall system reliability.

PowerShell's integration with SQL Server also extends to SQL Server Integration Services (SSIS) and SQL Server Reporting Services (SSRS), enabling administrators to automate the execution and management of SSIS packages and SSRS reports. The Invoke-SSISPackage cmdlet allows DBAs to run SSIS packages from PowerShell scripts, which can be scheduled as part of an ETL (Extract, Transform, Load) process. Similarly, PowerShell can be used to automate the generation and delivery of SSRS reports, sending reports via email or saving them to specific locations. This automation helps streamline business processes and ensures that data integration and reporting tasks are performed consistently and on time.

Another powerful aspect of SQL Server and PowerShell integration is the ability to work with SQL Server in virtualized and cloud environments. PowerShell allows administrators to manage SQL Server instances running on virtual machines (VMs) in platforms such as Hyper-V, VMware, and Microsoft Azure. PowerShell can be used to automate tasks such as provisioning VMs, configuring storage, and managing network settings, providing a unified approach to managing both the infrastructure and the SQL Server instances running on it. In cloud environments, PowerShell scripts can be used to automate the deployment, scaling, and monitoring of SQL Server instances on platforms like Microsoft Azure SQL Database and SQL Server on Azure Virtual Machines.

In complex SQL Server environments with multiple instances, automating routine tasks such as backups, security checks, and performance monitoring is essential for maintaining consistency and reducing administrative overhead. PowerShell scripts can be scheduled to run automatically on a regular basis, providing administrators with the flexibility to focus on more strategic tasks. Additionally, PowerShell's integration with other Microsoft tools, such as System Center, allows DBAs to manage SQL Server environments at scale, automating processes across multiple servers and instances.

Incorporating PowerShell into SQL Server administration offers a powerful way to enhance productivity, streamline management tasks, and reduce the potential for human error. By automating routine tasks such as backups, restores, security management, and performance monitoring, DBAs can ensure that SQL Server environments run efficiently and remain secure. Furthermore, PowerShell's ability to integrate with other Microsoft technologies provides a comprehensive solution for managing the full lifecycle of SQL Server instances, from installation to monitoring and troubleshooting. By leveraging the full capabilities of PowerShell, organizations can optimize their SQL Server management processes, reduce operational costs, and improve system performance.

# Upgrading and Patching SQL Server

Upgrading and patching SQL Server are critical aspects of database administration that help maintain system performance, security, and functionality. As SQL Server evolves, new features, enhancements, and bug fixes are introduced with each version and update. While the process of upgrading and patching might seem straightforward, it requires careful planning, testing, and execution to avoid disruptions, ensure compatibility, and minimize downtime. Effective management of upgrades and patches ensures that organizations continue to benefit from the latest improvements in SQL Server, while also mitigating the risks associated with outdated software, such as security vulnerabilities or poor performance.

Upgrading SQL Server typically involves moving from an older version to a newer version, such as from SQL Server 2014 to SQL Server 2019. This process can introduce new features that improve performance, scalability, and security, but it also requires a thoughtful approach to avoid potential issues that may arise during the migration. The first step in any SQL Server upgrade is to assess the environment to determine the feasibility of the upgrade. This involves evaluating the current version of SQL Server, understanding the applications that rely on the database, and identifying any dependencies or custom configurations that might be affected by the upgrade. For example, certain features that are deprecated or removed in newer versions of SQL Server may require changes to applications or scripts that interact with the database.

Before performing the upgrade, it is essential to back up all databases, including system databases like the master, model, and msdb databases. This ensures that if something goes wrong during the upgrade, administrators can restore the databases to their previous state. It is also advisable to perform the upgrade in a test environment before applying it to production systems. This allows DBAs to verify that the upgrade will not cause issues with existing applications, custom stored procedures, or other critical components. During this testing phase, administrators should use tools such as SQL Server's Data Migration Assistant (DMA) to check for compatibility issues, deprecated features, and breaking changes between the old and new versions. The DMA can help identify problems early in the process, allowing for adjustments before the upgrade takes place.

Once the testing phase is complete and the upgrade plan has been validated, administrators can proceed with the upgrade process. SQL Server provides several methods for upgrading, including in-place upgrades, side-by-side upgrades, and the use of SQL Server's backup and restore functionality. An in-place upgrade involves upgrading the existing SQL Server instance directly, without moving the data to a new server. While this method is quicker, it carries the risk of leaving behind legacy configurations and is not recommended for complex environments or large-scale databases. A side-by-side upgrade, on the other hand, involves installing the new version of SQL Server on a separate server and migrating the databases to the new instance. This approach allows for a smoother transition, as it preserves the old environment and allows for testing and troubleshooting before decommissioning the old server.

Another approach to upgrading SQL Server is through the use of backup and restore operations. This method involves backing up the databases from the old instance and restoring them to the new instance. This approach can be used for both in-place and side-by-side upgrades and offers a reliable way to migrate data without impacting the source environment. It is important to ensure that the new server has adequate hardware resources and configurations that meet the requirements of the new version of SQL Server, as newer versions may have different resource demands than older ones.

Patching SQL Server is a continuous process that involves applying updates released by Microsoft to address security vulnerabilities, improve system stability, and fix bugs. Unlike upgrades, which are major version changes, patches are smaller updates that are designed to address specific issues within the current version of SQL Server. Patching is essential to keeping SQL Server secure and running efficiently. Microsoft releases service packs, cumulative updates, and security updates to address issues discovered after a SQL Server version has been released. These patches should be installed regularly, especially security updates, as they help protect SQL Server from potential exploits.

The first step in patching SQL Server is to identify the patches that are applicable to the installed version of SQL Server. SQL Server supports multiple versions, and the available patches depend on the version and edition in use. Administrators can use the SQL Server setup program or the Microsoft Update tool to identify and download the necessary patches. It is essential to review the release notes and documentation associated with each patch to understand what changes or fixes the patch includes and to ensure that it will not interfere with the current environment.

Before applying any patch, administrators should back up the databases and SQL Server system databases to ensure that they can recover the system in case something goes wrong during the patching process. The patching process itself can be automated using SQL Server Agent or PowerShell scripts to apply updates on a schedule. However, it is often recommended to apply patches during a maintenance window to minimize disruption to users. During the patching process, SQL Server may restart, and services may temporarily become unavailable, so it is essential to notify stakeholders and ensure that appropriate measures are in place to handle any disruptions.

Once the patch has been applied, administrators should test the system to ensure that SQL Server is functioning properly. This includes verifying that the databases are accessible, that performance has not been negatively impacted, and that any new features or fixes included in the patch are functioning as expected. Administrators should also check the SQL Server error logs for any unusual activity or errors that may have occurred during the patching process. If any issues are detected, the system can be rolled back to the previous state using the backup taken before the patch was applied.

Regular patching is essential for maintaining the security and stability of SQL Server, but it requires careful planning and monitoring to ensure that the process is completed without issues. One best practice is to implement a patch management process that includes testing patches in a staging environment before applying them to production systems. This helps to identify potential issues before they affect the live system. Additionally, administrators should regularly check for new updates and apply them as part of a proactive maintenance schedule to keep the SQL Server environment up to date.

In some cases, patching may also require changes to SQL Server configurations or hardware resources, especially when new features or performance enhancements are introduced in the patches. It is important for administrators to stay informed about the latest developments in SQL Server and to evaluate the impact of patches on the overall system. By staying up to date with patching and upgrading, organizations can ensure that SQL Server continues to perform at its best, remains secure, and benefits from the latest features and optimizations.

Managing SQL Server upgrades and patches is a critical part of ensuring that the database environment remains stable, secure, and optimized for performance. While the process can be complex and requires careful planning, it is essential for maintaining a healthy SQL Server infrastructure. By following best practices for upgrades and patching, DBAs can minimize downtime, reduce the risk of errors, and ensure that SQL Server continues to meet the needs of the organization. Through regular updates and upgrades, SQL Server administrators can maintain a secure, reliable, and high-performance database environment.

# SQL Server Maintenance Plans and Best Practices

SQL Server maintenance is essential for ensuring that databases run smoothly, securely, and efficiently. Without regular maintenance, SQL Server instances can experience performance degradation, reliability issues, or even data loss. Establishing comprehensive maintenance plans and adhering to best practices is crucial for the longevity and health of the SQL Server environment. Maintenance plans help database administrators (DBAs) automate routine tasks such as backups, integrity checks, index optimization, and performance monitoring. By automating these tasks, administrators can reduce human error, ensure consistency, and free up time for more strategic initiatives. In this chapter, we will explore the key elements of SQL Server maintenance plans, the best practices for implementing them, and how they contribute to a stable and performant database environment.

One of the cornerstones of any SQL Server maintenance plan is regular database backups. Backups are the most important safeguard against data loss and corruption, making it critical for administrators to set up an effective backup strategy. A good maintenance plan should incorporate full, differential, and transaction log backups at scheduled intervals to ensure that data can be restored in the event of failure. Full backups should be taken periodically, depending on the size and activity of the database. Differential backups, which capture only changes made since the last full backup, are typically scheduled more frequently to minimize the time and space required for backup operations. Transaction log backups are essential for point-in-time recovery and should be performed as often as necessary based on the transaction volume. By automating these backups within a maintenance plan, administrators can ensure that data is consistently protected and that recovery procedures can be executed smoothly when needed.

Another critical task in a maintenance plan is running integrity checks on databases. SQL Server databases are susceptible to corruption due to various factors, such as hardware failures, power outages, or software bugs. Running regular integrity checks using the DBCC CHECKDB command helps identify corruption early and prevents potential issues from escalating. It is recommended to schedule integrity checks during off-peak hours to minimize the impact on server performance. These checks can be automated through SQL Server Agent jobs, which ensure that the process runs on a consistent schedule without manual intervention. By including integrity checks as part of the maintenance plan, DBAs can ensure that databases are in a healthy state and free from logical and physical corruption.

Index optimization is another key component of a comprehensive maintenance plan. Over time, as data is inserted, updated, or deleted, indexes can become fragmented, leading to poor query performance. Index fragmentation occurs when the logical order of data in an index does not match the physical order, resulting in increased I/O and slower query execution. To prevent this, SQL Server provides tools for reorganizing and rebuilding indexes. Reorganizing indexes is less resource-intensive and can be done more frequently, while rebuilding indexes provides a more thorough optimization but requires more system resources. Index optimization tasks can be automated by setting up maintenance plans to reorganize or rebuild indexes based on fragmentation levels. Running these tasks regularly ensures that indexes remain efficient, helping SQL Server execute queries more quickly and improving overall system performance.

SQL Server maintenance plans should also include statistics updates. SQL Server uses statistics to estimate query execution plans and determine the most efficient way to retrieve data. Outdated or inaccurate statistics can lead to suboptimal query plans, resulting in poor performance. By automatically updating statistics as part of the maintenance plan, administrators can ensure that SQL Server's query optimizer has the most up-to-date information, improving query performance. The frequency of statistics updates should be based on the rate of data changes and the complexity of queries. In highly dynamic environments where data changes frequently, updating statistics more regularly is crucial for maintaining query performance.

Another essential maintenance task is ensuring that SQL Server has sufficient storage and that log files are properly managed. Over time, SQL Server databases can grow, leading to storage constraints. Regular monitoring of disk space usage and the size of database files is necessary to prevent issues with disk capacity. Maintenance plans should include tasks to check for available disk space, shrink data files if needed, and ensure that transaction log files are appropriately sized and truncated. It is also recommended to regularly monitor the tempdb database, as it plays a key role in SQL Server's temporary storage for operations like sorting and hashing. If tempdb grows too large, it can impact performance, so managing its size and ensuring that it has sufficient resources is critical.

Performance monitoring is another crucial aspect of SQL Server maintenance. Maintaining optimal performance requires regular assessment of SQL Server's health and identifying potential bottlenecks. Performance monitoring tasks should be included in the maintenance plan to track key performance metrics such as CPU usage, memory utilization, disk I/O, and query performance. SQL Server provides dynamic management views (DMVs) that offer insights into system performance and can be queried to identify problematic queries or resource-intensive operations. Automating performance monitoring within the maintenance plan ensures that any issues are detected promptly and can be addressed before they affect end-users. Additionally, capturing performance data over time can help DBAs identify trends, plan for capacity upgrades, and optimize resource allocation.

Security is an essential consideration in any SQL Server maintenance plan. Regular maintenance tasks should include checking security settings, verifying user access, and auditing SQL Server logins and roles. SQL Server environments should follow the principle of least privilege, ensuring that users only have access to the data and functionality they need to perform their tasks. Regularly reviewing and updating security policies, password policies, and login configurations helps protect against unauthorized access and potential breaches. Security patches and updates should be applied promptly to address vulnerabilities and ensure that SQL Server remains protected against known threats. These security tasks should be automated and incorporated into the overall maintenance plan to ensure that the environment remains secure.

In addition to routine maintenance tasks, the plan should include disaster recovery and failover testing. Regular testing of backup and recovery procedures is crucial for ensuring that databases can be restored quickly and accurately in the event of a failure. Testing restores should be done periodically to verify the integrity of backup files and ensure that recovery operations can be executed smoothly. For high-availability environments, maintenance plans should include tasks to verify the status of failover clustering or AlwaysOn Availability

Groups to ensure that failover mechanisms are functioning as expected.

While SQL Server provides a variety of built-in tools for managing maintenance, it is essential for administrators to monitor and optimize these processes continuously. Regular audits of maintenance tasks, performance, and system health help ensure that SQL Server runs optimally and remains aligned with organizational needs. Setting up comprehensive maintenance plans allows DBAs to automate repetitive tasks, reduce administrative overhead, and ensure that SQL Server remains in peak condition, ready to meet the demands of users and applications.

SQL Server maintenance plans and best practices are integral to ensuring the health and performance of database environments. By incorporating routine tasks such as backups, integrity checks, index optimization, performance monitoring, and security management, administrators can safeguard their systems against data loss, performance degradation, and security vulnerabilities. Automation of these tasks through SQL Server Agent jobs and scripts not only reduces human error but also ensures consistency and reliability in database operations. A well-structured maintenance plan, coupled with ongoing monitoring and adjustments, forms the foundation for a stable, high-performing SQL Server environment.

# Data and Transaction Security in SQL Server

Data and transaction security are paramount concerns for any organization using SQL Server as their relational database management system (RDBMS). Given the critical nature of the data stored in SQL Server, safeguarding this data from unauthorized access, corruption, and loss is essential for maintaining confidentiality, integrity, and availability. SQL Server provides a robust set of security features that allow database administrators (DBAs) to enforce strict access controls, monitor user activities, and ensure the protection of sensitive information. In addition to securing the data itself, securing transactions within SQL Server is equally important, as transactions represent the core of data manipulation, ensuring that operations are completed reliably and without interference. This chapter explores the various mechanisms and strategies available in SQL Server for protecting both data and transactions, focusing on authentication, authorization, encryption, auditing, and transaction management.

SQL Server uses multiple layers of security to ensure data protection. One of the fundamental aspects of data security is access control. SQL Server provides two modes of authentication: Windows Authentication and SQL Server Authentication. Windows Authentication is the most secure option because it integrates with the Active Directory (AD) infrastructure, leveraging centralized authentication and applying the organization's security policies. With Windows Authentication, SQL Server relies on the underlying Windows security infrastructure to validate users, ensuring that access is granted only to those who have been authenticated by the domain. SQL Server Authentication, on the other hand, is a standalone method where users must supply a username and password specific to SQL Server. While SQL Server Authentication can be used for scenarios where Active Directory is not available, it is generally considered less secure than Windows Authentication, especially when dealing with complex environments.

In addition to authentication, SQL Server also provides a sophisticated model for authorization. Authorization determines what a user or group of users is allowed to do once they have been authenticated. This is managed through SQL Server logins, users, and roles. A login grants access to SQL Server, and once a login is created, a user account is mapped to it within specific databases. Permissions are then granted to users or roles, which determine the level of access to specific database objects, such as tables, views, and stored procedures. SQL Server implements the principle of least privilege, meaning that users should only be given the permissions they need to perform their jobs and nothing more. This reduces the attack surface by limiting the ability of unauthorized users to perform actions outside of their role. For sensitive operations, such as modifying data or managing security, SQL Server allows the creation of custom roles with tailored permissions, giving DBAs fine-grained control over who can do what.

Another important aspect of data security in SQL Server is encryption. Encryption helps protect sensitive data both at rest (on disk) and in transit (over the network). SQL Server provides several encryption options, with Transparent Data Encryption (TDE) being one of the most widely used for protecting data at rest. TDE encrypts the entire database, including its backups, preventing unauthorized access to the data even if the database files are stolen. TDE operates at the database level and requires minimal changes to the application or SQL Server configuration. For data in transit, SQL Server supports Secure Sockets Layer (SSL) and Transport Layer Security (TLS) encryption to secure communications between SQL Server instances and clients. By enabling SSL/TLS, data transmitted over the network is encrypted, preventing man-in-the-middle attacks and eavesdropping on sensitive information as it moves between clients and the server.

SQL Server also provides fine-grained encryption options at the column level using Always Encrypted. This feature enables the encryption of specific columns that contain sensitive information, such as credit card numbers or social security numbers, ensuring that only authorized applications or users can access the plaintext values. Always Encrypted ensures that the encryption keys are never exposed to SQL Server, which means that even DBAs cannot view the sensitive data directly. This adds an additional layer of security, especially for organizations that handle personally identifiable information (PII) or other confidential data.

To further strengthen transaction security, SQL Server uses a transaction-based model that guarantees data consistency, reliability, and durability through the ACID (Atomicity, Consistency, Isolation, Durability) properties. SQL Server ensures that transactions are completed in full or rolled back if any part of the transaction fails, thereby preventing partial or inconsistent data changes. SQL Server uses the transaction log to record all changes made to the database, which ensures that in the event of a system failure, SQL Server can recover to a consistent state. The transaction log also helps with auditing and compliance by providing a complete record of database changes.

SQL Server implements several transaction isolation levels to control how transactions interact with each other. The isolation level defines the visibility of changes made by one transaction to other transactions that are running concurrently. The higher the isolation level, the more stringent the data consistency guarantees, but this can also reduce concurrency and increase locking. SQL Server provides four main isolation levels: Read Uncommitted, Read Committed, Repeatable Read, and Serializable. Each isolation level offers a different balance between performance and data consistency, allowing DBAs to choose the appropriate level based on the specific needs of their applications. For example, the Read Committed isolation level, which is the default, ensures that transactions can only read committed data, preventing dirty reads, but still allows for other types of concurrency issues like non-repeatable reads.

For environments that require high levels of concurrency and transactional integrity, SQL Server also supports the use of optimistic concurrency control through features such as snapshot isolation. Snapshot isolation provides each transaction with a consistent snapshot of the data at the beginning of the transaction, allowing for higher concurrency without the need for locks. This is especially useful in systems where there are frequent reads and occasional writes, and locking would severely impact performance.

In addition to these security and transaction management features, SQL Server provides robust auditing capabilities that enable DBAs to track and log activities within the database. SQL Server Audit allows administrators to monitor and log a wide range of actions, including user login attempts, changes to database objects, and data modifications. By auditing these activities, organizations can ensure compliance with regulatory requirements and detect unauthorized access or suspicious activities. SQL Server logs can be stored in dedicated audit files or forwarded to external monitoring systems for centralized tracking and analysis.

Regular security reviews, patching, and updates are also essential for maintaining the integrity and protection of SQL Server environments. SQL Server releases security patches and updates periodically to address vulnerabilities that could be exploited by attackers. It is critical to apply these updates promptly to minimize the risk of security breaches. In addition to patching, regular security assessments and vulnerability scans should be performed to identify potential risks and ensure that SQL Server environments remain secure.

SQL Server's security features provide a multi-layered approach to protecting data and transactions. By implementing robust authentication, authorization, encryption, and auditing practices, DBAs can safeguard SQL Server environments against unauthorized access, data corruption, and other security threats. Moreover, SQL Server's transaction management capabilities ensure that data remains consistent and reliable, even in the face of system failures or concurrent transactions. Through a combination of these security measures and ongoing best practices, organizations can ensure that their SQL Server instances remain protected, secure, and compliant with industry standards.

# Auditing SQL Server for Compliance and Security

Auditing SQL Server environments is a critical part of maintaining compliance with industry regulations and ensuring the overall security of data assets. Modern organizations rely heavily on SQL Server to store and manage sensitive data, making it a prime target for both internal misuse and external attacks. As such, establishing comprehensive auditing mechanisms is not only a best practice but also a requirement under frameworks such as GDPR, HIPAA, SOX, and PCI DSS. The process of auditing SQL Server involves tracking and recording events related to data access, modifications, and configuration changes in order to provide accountability and support forensic analysis in the event of a breach or policy violation.

The foundation of any SQL Server audit strategy begins with defining the scope of what needs to be audited. This typically includes actions performed by privileged users such as database administrators, changes to database schemas, and access to sensitive tables containing personally identifiable information or financial records. While SQL Server provides several built-in mechanisms for auditing, including SQL Server Audit, Change Data Capture (CDC), and server and database-level triggers, the choice of which to use often depends on organizational requirements, regulatory demands, and performance considerations. SQL Server Audit, introduced in SQL Server 2008, is the most robust and compliant-friendly feature available. It allows administrators to create audit specifications that log actions at both the server and database levels, capturing fine-grained events such as login attempts, data modifications, and permission changes.

A well-designed auditing implementation involves creating and configuring audit objects like audit specifications and audit targets. These targets define where the audit logs will be stored, whether in application logs, the Windows Security log, or dedicated audit files. Choosing the correct destination is vital for preserving the integrity and confidentiality of audit data. Storing audit logs in the Windows Security log, for instance, provides tamper-evident protection and can integrate with existing SIEM (Security Information and Event Management) solutions, enabling real-time analysis and alerting. However, writing to the Windows Security log requires elevated permissions and may impact performance if not properly managed. Dedicated audit files, on the other hand, offer flexibility and can be archived and retained for longer periods to meet compliance retention requirements.

In addition to selecting appropriate audit targets, administrators must carefully define the audit actions and groups to be monitored. This includes events like SELECT, INSERT, UPDATE, and DELETE operations on sensitive tables, as well as security-related actions such as granting or revoking privileges. Monitoring login attempts and failed authentication efforts is essential for detecting potential brute-force attacks or unauthorized access attempts. Equally important is the auditing of schema modifications, as changes to table structures or stored procedures may indicate tampering or unauthorized development activity. Capturing these events not only helps in tracing accountability but also aids in understanding the impact of changes on application behavior and performance.

Audit data must be reviewed regularly, and alerts should be configured for critical events such as unauthorized access to confidential data or privilege escalation. Relying on manual log inspection is impractical in large-scale environments, so automation through SQL Server Agent jobs, PowerShell scripts, or third-party auditing tools is often necessary. These tools can parse audit logs, flag anomalies, and generate reports for compliance auditors. Some advanced solutions offer correlation across multiple databases and servers, identifying suspicious patterns that may indicate insider threats or lateral movement by attackers. The ability to visualize audit trails through dashboards enhances situational awareness and enables faster response to incidents.

Security of audit data is as important as the data itself. Audit logs must be protected from unauthorized access and tampering to preserve their integrity and evidentiary value. Role-based access controls should restrict who can read, modify, or delete audit logs, and all audit-related configurations should be documented and version-controlled. Encrypting audit files and using secure transmission protocols when exporting logs to external systems are additional measures that strengthen security posture. Backup strategies for audit logs should align with overall disaster recovery plans to ensure that historical data is not lost in the event of system failure.

Periodic audit reviews should be conducted to assess the effectiveness of the auditing strategy. These reviews may identify gaps in coverage, such as tables or actions that were not originally included but have become sensitive due to evolving business requirements. Auditing should be adaptive, not static. Changes in regulatory standards or organizational policies may necessitate updates to audit specifications. Moreover, performance impacts of auditing should be monitored continuously. Excessive logging or poorly scoped audits can degrade system responsiveness, so administrators must balance security and compliance with system performance and availability.

Auditing is not limited to technical configurations; it must be supported by governance policies and operational procedures. Clear guidelines should exist around what events are to be audited, how long logs are retained, who is responsible for review, and how anomalies are escalated. Training staff on the importance of auditing and how to interpret audit data is vital for building a security-conscious culture. In regulated industries, audit readiness is a constant concern, and being able to demonstrate a consistent, well-documented audit trail is essential during inspections and audits by external authorities.

In summary, auditing SQL Server for compliance and security is a multifaceted endeavor that blends technical controls, organizational policies, and continuous oversight. It ensures that actions taken within the database environment are recorded, monitored, and reviewed, forming a critical component of any data protection strategy. As threats become more sophisticated and compliance standards more stringent, organizations must invest in robust auditing practices to safeguard their SQL Server environments and maintain trust with customers, partners, and regulators.

# Implementing SQL Server Reporting and Analysis Tools

Implementing SQL Server reporting and analysis tools is a cornerstone of modern business intelligence strategies. SQL Server provides a rich set of integrated services designed to transform raw data into actionable insights through reporting, visualization, and analytical capabilities. These services include SQL Server Reporting Services (SSRS), SQL Server Analysis Services (SSAS), and Power BI integration. Together, they form a comprehensive ecosystem for organizations to generate reports, perform multidimensional and tabular analysis, and make data-driven decisions. The implementation of these tools requires a strategic approach that encompasses infrastructure planning, data modeling, report design, security configurations, and performance optimization.

SQL Server Reporting Services is the primary platform for building, managing, and delivering paginated reports. SSRS enables the development of pixel-perfect reports that can be rendered in multiple formats including PDF, Excel, Word, and HTML. The implementation process begins with setting up the SSRS server, which can be installed in native or SharePoint-integrated mode, depending on the organization's collaboration and portal requirements. Native mode remains the most common due to its simplicity and independence from additional infrastructure. Once SSRS is installed and configured, report developers use SQL Server Data Tools or Report Builder to design reports by connecting to data sources, writing queries, and laying out data regions such as tables, matrices, and charts. Reports can include parameters for dynamic filtering, expressions for conditional formatting, and custom code for advanced logic.

Effective use of SSRS depends on thoughtful data modeling. While SSRS can query databases directly using T-SQL, performance and maintainability are improved when reports are built on top of views or stored procedures. This encapsulates the business logic within the database, enabling reuse and reducing the risk of inconsistencies across reports. Report deployment involves publishing reports to the report server where they are organized into folders, assigned permissions, and configured for execution or subscription. SSRS supports scheduled report delivery through email or file shares, allowing users to receive data on a recurring basis without manual intervention. It also provides a web portal for interactive viewing and management of reports.

In parallel with SSRS, SQL Server Analysis Services offers powerful capabilities for multidimensional and tabular data analysis. SSAS allows organizations to build analytical models that pre-aggregate data and expose it in a format optimized for exploration and reporting. The multidimensional model, based on OLAP cubes, provides rich hierarchies, measures, and dimensions that enable slicing and dicing of data from different perspectives. The tabular model, introduced in newer versions of SSAS, uses in-memory technology and columnar storage to deliver high-performance analytics with a simpler development experience. The implementation of SSAS begins with designing a data source view, followed by defining dimensions and measures that align with business metrics.

A well-implemented SSAS solution supports advanced analytics such as time-based calculations, key performance indicators (KPIs), and user hierarchies. Security within SSAS is enforced through role-based access, allowing developers to define what data each user can see based on their role. After deployment, users can connect to SSAS models from Excel or Power BI to perform ad hoc analysis and create dashboards. Excel PivotTables and Power BI visualizations provide intuitive interfaces for interacting with SSAS data, making it accessible to both technical and non-technical users. The processing of SSAS models must be scheduled to ensure data freshness, which can be managed through SQL Server Agent jobs or integration with SQL Server Integration Services (SSIS).

Power BI adds another dimension to SQL Server's reporting and analysis capabilities by offering self-service BI and interactive dashboards. While Power BI is a separate product, it integrates seamlessly with SSRS and SSAS. Reports authored in Power BI Desktop can connect to on-premises SQL Server databases, SSAS models, and other data sources. With the use of gateways, organizations can maintain real-time or scheduled data refreshes for Power BI reports. Power BI also supports direct query and import modes, allowing flexibility based on the size of the dataset and performance requirements. The ability to publish Power BI reports to the Power BI Service enables collaboration, sharing, and mobile access, expanding the reach of BI content across the organization.

Implementing SQL Server reporting and analysis tools is not solely a technical endeavor but also involves governance and process alignment. Data governance ensures that the data being reported is accurate, timely, and consistent. Metadata management, naming conventions, version control, and documentation are essential for sustaining the reporting environment. User training and support are also critical for adoption. A reporting solution, no matter how powerful, fails to deliver value if users do not understand how to interpret and interact with the data. Therefore, organizations must invest in training programs, user guides, and help desk support to maximize the benefits of their reporting infrastructure.

Performance tuning is a recurring theme in the implementation of SQL Server reporting and analysis tools. Poorly written queries, unoptimized data models, and excessive data retrieval can slow down report generation and degrade user experience. Indexing strategies, partitioning, and query optimization play key roles in ensuring responsiveness. Caching mechanisms in SSRS and SSAS can further improve performance by reusing precomputed results. Monitoring tools and logging features within SQL Server help identify bottlenecks and usage patterns, informing future enhancements.

Security is a paramount consideration throughout the implementation. Access to reports and analytical models must be carefully controlled to protect sensitive information. This includes configuring permissions at the report server, database, and model levels. Encryption of data in transit, secure storage of credentials, and auditing of user activity are necessary to comply with security standards and prevent data leaks. Integration with Active Directory facilitates centralized user management and simplifies the enforcement of access policies.

Implementing SQL Server reporting and analysis tools creates a scalable and secure foundation for enterprise-wide business intelligence. When properly architected and maintained, these tools empower users to make informed decisions, discover trends, and respond proactively to changes in the business environment. Whether delivering static reports or enabling dynamic exploration of multidimensional models, SQL Server's ecosystem of reporting and analysis services supports the full spectrum of BI needs across departments and industries. SQL Server Resource Governance and Management

SQL Server Resource Governance and Management is a critical component in maintaining a balanced and efficient database environment, particularly in scenarios where multiple workloads coexist on the same SQL Server instance. As modern enterprises increasingly consolidate systems and applications, it becomes imperative to ensure that no single workload monopolizes resources to the detriment of others. SQL Server provides several tools and mechanisms to manage CPU, memory, and I/O distribution, ensuring that all operations maintain acceptable performance levels even under pressure. This chapter explores how SQL Server achieves this and why such resource governance is vital for both stability and scalability.

Resource Governor is the central feature introduced in SQL Server to address the issue of workload management. It allows database administrators to classify sessions based on pre-defined criteria and allocate resources accordingly. These classifications are made using user-defined functions that analyze incoming session attributes such as application name, login name, or host name. Once a session is classified, it is assigned to a resource pool via a workload group. Each resource pool is configured with minimum and maximum thresholds for CPU usage and memory grants, enabling SQL Server to impose limits and prevent runaway queries from exhausting system resources.

One of the most powerful aspects of Resource Governor is its ability to enforce predictable performance across different types of workloads. For example, a reporting application generating long-running analytical queries can be placed in a pool with limited CPU and memory, ensuring that transactional workloads for online users are not delayed. Similarly, batch processing jobs that execute during off-peak hours can be throttled during business hours and given more generous resources later. This dynamic allocation allows for a fine-tuned balance that maximizes overall throughput without compromising critical real-time operations.

Resource Governor settings are not static and can be altered to accommodate changing business needs. Administrators can modify resource pool definitions or workload group assignments as usage patterns evolve. Additionally, SQL Server supports monitoring of resource pool performance through dynamic management views, which provide real-time insights into how resources are being consumed. These views help detect bottlenecks and guide optimization efforts by highlighting which queries or sessions are placing excessive demand on particular system components.

Beyond CPU and memory control, SQL Server also includes mechanisms for managing I/O and tempdb usage. While Resource Governor does not directly control disk I/O in its current versions, administrators can architect solutions that isolate heavy I/O consumers by placing their data and log files on dedicated disks or storage arrays. Tempdb, being a shared resource used by all sessions, is another potential bottleneck. SQL Server offers configuration options like multiple tempdb files and trace flags to reduce contention and ensure equitable access among users and applications.

Effective resource management also involves setting up appropriate query execution plans and indexing strategies to minimize resource consumption. SQL Server's query optimizer plays a crucial role in this area by selecting efficient execution paths. However, it is up to the administrator to ensure that statistics are up to date and indexes are properly maintained. When poorly written queries or suboptimal plans are allowed to run unchecked, they can consume disproportionate resources, leading to degraded performance across the entire system. Proactive governance thus entails both automated resource allocation and diligent performance tuning.

Another important facet of SQL Server resource governance is integration with operating system-level tools. Features like Windows System Resource Manager (WSRM), now deprecated, previously allowed admins to enforce OS-level resource limits. Today, Windows Job Objects or virtualization environments like Hyper-V and VMware provide similar capabilities. SQL Server can be hosted in virtual machines with assigned CPU and memory caps, complementing the internal resource governance mechanisms and offering an additional layer of control.

SQL Server also supports affinity configuration, where administrators can bind specific workloads or processes to certain CPU cores. This can be useful in scenarios where certain operations need dedicated computational capacity. Coupled with NUMA-aware memory management, this level of control ensures efficient resource utilization, especially on servers with large core counts or complex memory architectures. While affinity settings should be approached with caution, they can offer significant benefits in high-performance or multi-tenant environments.

Resource governance is not solely about restriction; it is also about enabling fairness and prioritization. SQL Server includes capabilities to detect and handle deadlocks, prevent excessive locking, and manage concurrency in a way that promotes system health. Lock escalation thresholds, transaction isolation levels, and row versioning are all tools that help maintain responsiveness even under high load. These settings indirectly influence how resources are consumed and should be factored into any comprehensive resource management strategy.

As organizations adopt cloud-based deployments such as Azure SQL Database and Managed Instances, resource governance takes on new dimensions. These services abstract much of the underlying infrastructure, but they still offer tiers and elastic pools that emulate traditional resource pools. Administrators must still classify workloads, allocate budgets, and monitor performance to ensure optimal operation. While the tools may differ, the core principles of resource governance remain constant: balance, fairness, and predictability.

SQL Server Resource Governance and Management is not a one-time setup but an ongoing discipline that adapts to the evolving demands of users and applications. It requires a deep understanding of workload characteristics, business priorities, and system capabilities. By leveraging features like Resource Governor, intelligent monitoring, and strategic planning, database professionals can ensure that SQL Server remains responsive, resilient, and ready to meet the challenges of today's data-driven world.

# Managing SQL Server on Linux

Managing SQL Server on Linux represents a significant shift in the traditional landscape of database administration. For decades, SQL Server was tightly coupled with the Windows operating system, which limited its deployment scenarios and dictated specific administrative tools and methodologies. With the introduction of SQL Server for Linux, Microsoft opened new possibilities for organizations seeking to leverage open-source platforms while retaining the power and familiarity of SQL Server. The Linux version is not a limited subset but a full-fledged implementation of the SQL Server database engine, reengineered to run natively on Linux using the same core codebase as its Windows counterpart. This chapter explores the nuances, challenges, and advantages of managing SQL Server in a Linux environment and how it influences the day-to-day operations of database professionals.

One of the first notable differences when managing SQL Server on Linux is the command-line-centric nature of the operating system. Unlike Windows, where graphical interfaces like SQL Server Management Studio dominate administrative tasks, Linux relies more heavily on terminal-based operations. Administrators often interact with the database engine using tools like sqlcmd, Bash scripts, systemctl, and text-based configuration files. While this may initially seem daunting to those accustomed to graphical tools, it offers a level of precision, automation, and scripting capability that is ideal for modern DevOps practices. Moreover, the integration with native Linux logging systems such as journald and syslog provides new ways to monitor the SQL Server service and capture runtime diagnostics.

Installation and configuration on Linux follow a different path compared to Windows environments. SQL Server packages are distributed via platform-specific package managers, such as apt for Debian-based systems and yum or dnf for Red Hat-based systems. This allows for seamless updates, dependency tracking, and standardized installation procedures. After installing the database engine, configuration is typically completed using the mssql-conf tool, which enables the setting of options such as TCP port numbers, memory limits, and file locations. These settings can also be scripted and version-controlled, providing consistency across multiple deployments and facilitating reproducible environments, particularly in containerized or cloud-native infrastructures.

From a performance standpoint, SQL Server on Linux benefits from the lightweight nature of the host operating system. Linux generally consumes fewer system resources for background services, which can lead to improved performance and greater resource availability for the database engine. However, administrators must pay close attention to file system choices, I/O scheduler configurations, and kernel parameters to ensure optimal operation. SQL Server supports ext4 and XFS file systems, with recommendations varying depending on the workload type and storage hardware. Proper tuning of the disk subsystem, including alignment of data files and use of mount options like noatime, can lead to noticeable performance gains.

Security management in SQL Server on Linux also requires a shift in perspective. While the database engine retains core security features such as authentication modes, roles, and encryption, the underlying Linux permissions model introduces additional layers of control. File and directory permissions must be carefully set to prevent unauthorized access to sensitive data, configuration files, and logs. Furthermore, integration with Active Directory is possible through the use of Kerberos and LDAP, allowing for centralized identity management even in mixed environments. Security practices must also extend to the shell environment, ensuring that only authorized users can execute administrative commands or access protected directories.

Patching and upgrades in Linux follow a predictable and streamlined process, thanks to the use of package managers. Updates to SQL Server are published as updated packages, which can be downloaded and installed using standard tools. This approach reduces the complexity and downtime traditionally associated with patching on Windows systems. Additionally, backup and restore operations work consistently across platforms, allowing for cross-platform migration and disaster recovery scenarios. A database backed up on Windows can be restored on Linux and vice versa, providing flexibility in hybrid environments and easing the transition for organizations adopting Linux.

Monitoring and diagnostics are crucial for effective management, and SQL Server on Linux provides several tools to facilitate this. The dynamic management views (DMVs) are fully supported, enabling the same performance troubleshooting techniques used on Windows. Additionally, administrators can use Linux-native tools like top, iostat, vmstat, and sar to get insights into CPU, memory, and disk utilization. Combining these tools with SQL Server's built-in metrics allows for a comprehensive view of system health. Moreover, systemd integration ensures that the SQL Server service is properly managed during boot sequences, restarts automatically upon failure, and logs service-level messages in a structured and accessible format.

Automation plays a central role in managing SQL Server on Linux. The shell scripting environment enables administrators to create powerful scripts that can perform backup operations, apply configurations, monitor system health, and trigger alerts. Combined with tools like cron for scheduled tasks and Ansible for configuration management, these capabilities enable high levels of operational efficiency and reduce the risk of human error. Containerization using Docker or Podman further extends the possibilities, allowing SQL Server instances to be encapsulated in portable, self-contained environments that are easy to deploy, update, and scale.

Managing SQL Server on Linux also changes the dynamics of support and collaboration within IT teams. Linux system administrators, who may previously have had limited interaction with SQL Server, now become key stakeholders in its maintenance and performance. This fosters a more integrated operational model and encourages knowledge sharing across disciplines. Database administrators, in turn, expand their skill sets to include Linux command-line proficiency, system configuration, and open-source toolchains. This cross-functional expertise is essential in modern IT environments where agility and adaptability are paramount.

The move to SQL Server on Linux signifies more than a platform choice; it embodies a broader strategy of modernization, flexibility, and alignment with contemporary infrastructure trends. Whether deployed on bare metal, in virtual machines, or as part of a containerized microservices architecture, SQL Server on Linux brings the power of a proven relational database to the diverse and evolving ecosystem of enterprise computing. With the right knowledge, tooling, and practices, managing SQL Server on Linux can be not only feasible but highly rewarding for administrators seeking performance, stability, and innovation.

# SQL Server Disaster Recovery with Azure Integration

SQL Server disaster recovery has always been a critical component of enterprise database planning, but with the emergence of cloud technologies, particularly Microsoft Azure, the paradigm of how disaster recovery is implemented and managed has fundamentally changed. Organizations no longer have to rely solely on expensive secondary datacenters or complex, manually orchestrated failover processes. Instead, Azure offers a range of integrated services that allow SQL Server workloads to achieve high availability, geographic redundancy, and rapid recovery with greater simplicity and flexibility. Azure integration enhances traditional disaster recovery strategies by providing scalable, automated, and cost-effective options tailored to various business continuity requirements.

The foundation of any disaster recovery strategy is data replication and availability, and Azure extends this capability through services such as Azure Site Recovery, Azure Backup, and Always On Availability Groups deployed across hybrid or cloud-only architectures. Always On

Availability Groups, introduced in SQL Server 2012 and continuously improved in later versions, can be configured to span on-premises instances and Azure-based virtual machines. This means that a primary SQL Server instance running in a company's own datacenter can replicate its data to a secondary replica hosted in Azure. If a failure occurs at the primary site due to hardware failure, power outage, or natural disaster, traffic can be redirected to the Azure-based secondary, ensuring minimal downtime and continued service availability.

Azure also introduces the capability to host SQL Server databases as fully managed services through Azure SQL Database and Azure SQL Managed Instance. These offerings inherently include high availability and automated backups, and while they are not disaster recovery solutions in themselves, they reduce the administrative overhead typically associated with maintaining database infrastructure. Organizations can incorporate these services into their disaster recovery strategies by replicating critical workloads to Azure SQL services and using them as fallback platforms during major outages. This enables fast failover without requiring administrators to build and maintain full virtual machine replicas.

For virtual machine-based deployments, Azure offers built-in disaster recovery support through Azure Site Recovery. This service can replicate entire virtual machines, including SQL Server VMs, from on-premises Hyper-V or VMware environments to Azure. It allows replication frequency to be configured based on recovery point objectives, and it supports test failover, planned failover, and unplanned failover scenarios. By continuously synchronizing changes and providing recovery plans, Azure Site Recovery helps automate the orchestration of complex recovery processes, reducing human error and accelerating the time to recovery. In case of a disaster, administrators can fail over to the replicated virtual machine in Azure and resume operations with minimal impact.

Azure Backup complements Site Recovery by offering point-in-time backup solutions that protect databases, system states, and file structures. Unlike traditional backup systems that require local storage and manual off-site transfer, Azure Backup securely stores encrypted backups in the cloud, with options for long-term retention and compliance with various regulatory standards. SQL Server-specific backup integration is available through the Azure Backup agent or native SQL Server backup to URL functionality, which enables backups to be written directly to Azure Blob Storage. This not only provides geographic redundancy but also decouples backup storage from production environments, reducing the risk of data loss due to local corruption or sabotage.

Security and compliance are integral to any disaster recovery plan, and Azure provides a rich set of tools to meet these requirements. All data transferred to and from Azure is encrypted, and Azure's global infrastructure is built with strict compliance to certifications such as ISO 27001, HIPAA, and GDPR. Administrators can implement role-based access control, multi-factor authentication, and network isolation to ensure that only authorized personnel can access recovery environments and sensitive data. These features ensure that a disaster recovery plan not only restores data and services but does so in a way that preserves confidentiality and integrity.

Monitoring and alerting are also enhanced through Azure's integration with SQL Server. Azure Monitor, Log Analytics, and Application Insights can be configured to track the health of SQL Server workloads, alert administrators to failures or anomalies, and provide detailed telemetry that can be used to troubleshoot recovery operations. These tools feed into dashboards and incident response workflows that are essential for quickly diagnosing problems and initiating recovery actions. Furthermore, Azure Automation and Logic Apps can be used to script and orchestrate complex recovery steps, enabling automatic remediation and reducing the time it takes to execute a disaster recovery plan.

Testing disaster recovery plans is another area where Azure shines. Many organizations fail to regularly test their recovery processes due to the complexity and risk involved in disrupting live environments. Azure enables non-disruptive test failovers, allowing administrators to validate recovery procedures without impacting production systems. This ensures that recovery plans remain effective and up to date, especially as applications evolve and infrastructure changes. Regular testing improves confidence in disaster recovery readiness and helps identify gaps that might otherwise go unnoticed until a real disaster occurs.

Hybrid cloud models further enhance flexibility. By combining on-premises infrastructure with Azure's cloud capabilities, businesses can design custom recovery strategies that balance cost, performance, and risk. For example, an organization might choose to replicate only its most critical databases to Azure while maintaining local backups for less essential systems. Alternatively, the entire workload can be containerized and deployed in Kubernetes clusters that span both local and Azure nodes, enabling seamless failover across platforms. This modularity and scalability are key advantages of Azure's disaster recovery approach, empowering organizations to tailor their strategies based on specific operational and financial constraints.

SQL Server disaster recovery with Azure integration transforms how organizations plan for and respond to catastrophic failures. It offers the resilience of cloud infrastructure, the precision of automated orchestration, and the assurance of secure, compliant data handling. Through intelligent replication, managed services, cloud-native backup, and advanced monitoring, Azure empowers database administrators to build robust recovery strategies that align with modern expectations of uptime and service continuity. The result is a more agile, reliable, and cost-efficient disaster recovery posture that keeps SQL Server workloads protected in an increasingly unpredictable world.

# SQL Server Troubleshooting Tools and Techniques

SQL Server, like any complex software system, is prone to performance degradation, configuration errors, and unexpected failures. As such, effective troubleshooting is a core competency for any database administrator or support engineer. Troubleshooting involves identifying symptoms, isolating the root cause, and implementing solutions that restore performance and functionality without introducing new issues. Given the critical role SQL Server plays in most enterprise environments, efficient and accurate problem-solving techniques are essential to maintaining system availability and user satisfaction. SQL Server provides a wide range of built-in tools and features designed specifically to aid in troubleshooting, each tailored to detect different kinds of issues, from query slowdowns to memory pressure, I/O bottlenecks, blocking, deadlocks, and server-level failures.

One of the most powerful resources available to troubleshooters is the Dynamic Management Views, or DMVs. These internal views offer real-time insights into nearly every aspect of the SQL Server engine, including active sessions, memory allocations, query execution plans, I/O statistics, and wait types. By querying the appropriate DMVs, administrators can pinpoint which queries are consuming the most resources, identify sessions experiencing waits, and assess memory usage patterns that may indicate inefficient indexing or parameter sniffing issues. DMVs like sys.dm_exec_requests, sys.dm_exec_sessions, sys.dm_exec_query_stats, and sys.dm_os_wait_stats are commonly used to gather evidence during performance troubleshooting. These views are also essential for constructing baselines and monitoring ongoing trends, which can later help correlate anomalies to specific events or workloads.

Another essential tool is SQL Server Profiler, which allows administrators to trace database activity in real-time. Profiler captures a wide range of events such as batch completions, login attempts, deadlocks, and query executions. By filtering trace results and focusing on high-cost or error-producing queries, administrators can identify problematic code that may not surface through DMVs alone. Although Profiler has been largely superseded by Extended Events in modern SQL Server versions, it remains a familiar and occasionally useful tool, particularly when quick interactive tracing is required. However, its performance overhead must be considered, especially in production environments, where excessive tracing can lead to further performance degradation.

Extended Events provide a more efficient and scalable way to capture diagnostic information in SQL Server. Designed to replace SQL Trace and Profiler, Extended Events offer a lightweight architecture with granular control over event selection, data capture, and output formatting. With Extended Events, administrators can build custom sessions that collect specific event data based on filters, time windows, or resource thresholds. This enables precise targeting of problematic behaviors, such as long-running queries, excessive recompilations, or blocking chains. Extended Events integrate tightly with SQL Server Management Studio, allowing for graphical analysis and correlation of captured data. Because of their low overhead, they are suitable for both proactive monitoring and reactive troubleshooting.

When it comes to analyzing query performance, the execution plan is indispensable. Execution plans provide a roadmap of how SQL Server interprets and executes a query, including the steps taken, indexes used, joins performed, and estimated versus actual row counts. Viewing an actual execution plan can reveal whether SQL Server is using efficient access paths or resorting to full table scans and nested loop joins that degrade performance. Administrators can access these plans through Management Studio or by enabling the SHOWPLAN XML option in query sessions. By studying execution plans, it becomes possible to detect missing indexes, bad statistics, or suboptimal joins that cause resource contention. Understanding how to read and interpret these plans is a critical troubleshooting skill.

Blocking and deadlocking are common concurrency issues that can cause query slowdowns and application timeouts. Blocking occurs when one session holds a lock that another session needs, while deadlocks occur when two or more sessions wait indefinitely for each other's resources. SQL Server detects deadlocks automatically and resolves them by terminating one of the sessions, usually the one with the least processing cost. To investigate these scenarios, administrators use DMVs such as sys.dm_tran_locks and sys.dm_os_waiting_tasks, or they configure Extended Events to capture deadlock graphs. These graphs illustrate the involved sessions, resources, and lock types, helping administrators design strategies to minimize contention, such as reducing transaction scopes, adding appropriate indexes, or changing isolation levels.

The Error Log and Windows Event Log are also valuable resources for troubleshooting server-level problems. The SQL Server Error Log captures startup messages, failed logins, backup events, and critical errors. Reviewing these logs can help diagnose service crashes, failed jobs, or replication issues. The Windows Event Log complements this information by including system-level messages that may affect SQL Server, such as hardware errors, driver issues, or memory faults. Together, these logs provide a chronological view of server health and facilitate the correlation of incidents across layers of the infrastructure.

For storage-related issues, administrators rely on tools like sys.dm_io_virtual_file_stats, which displays latency, I/O counts, and throughput per database file. These statistics can be used to identify underperforming storage systems or misconfigured file structures. In scenarios involving tempdb contention, for instance, performance can degrade due to latch contention on system pages. Adding multiple tempdb data files and monitoring latch waits can mitigate this issue. Additionally, monitoring I/O patterns over time can reveal if certain workloads cause spikes in latency, prompting a reevaluation of indexing, partitioning, or data compression strategies.

Memory pressure and CPU saturation are other areas where troubleshooting is often required. SQL Server uses a buffer pool to manage memory efficiently, but under memory pressure, it may flush pages to disk more frequently or delay query execution. DMVs such as sys.dm_os_memory_clerks and sys.dm_os_sys_memory can be queried to detect memory allocation patterns, external memory pressure, and signs of paging. High CPU utilization, on the other hand, might be caused by inefficient queries, parallelism issues, or system-level processes. In such cases, sys.dm_exec_requests and sys.dm_exec_query_plan can help identify the culprits, while Resource Governor can be employed to throttle resource-heavy workloads.

SQL Server Agent jobs and integration services packages often play a role in scheduled operations, and failures in these components can disrupt business processes. Troubleshooting failed jobs involves reviewing the job history logs, enabling job step logging, and examining output files. Integration Services packages that fail to execute properly might require analysis of package logs, SSISDB catalog reports, and event handlers to detect configuration or data-related issues. Ensuring that jobs are scheduled during off-peak hours and that dependencies are managed properly can prevent cascading failures across systems.

Effective SQL Server troubleshooting requires a comprehensive understanding of how the engine operates, where to find critical diagnostic information, and how to interpret that information accurately. It involves not only technical skills but also analytical thinking, pattern recognition, and the discipline to gather sufficient data before implementing changes. By mastering the built-in tools and adopting a structured approach to diagnosis, administrators can resolve issues quickly and prevent future incidents, ensuring that SQL Server continues to support the demanding workloads of modern business environments.

# Designing Scalable SQL Server Architectures

Designing scalable SQL Server architectures is a fundamental discipline in enterprise database management, where the demands of data volume, concurrency, and performance evolve rapidly with the growth of applications and users. A scalable architecture ensures that SQL Server can efficiently handle increasing workloads without requiring a complete redesign of the system. It allows businesses to grow confidently, knowing their database infrastructure can support more data, more users, and more complex operations over time. The key to successful scalability lies in the combination of sound architectural planning, understanding workload characteristics, anticipating growth patterns, and making judicious use of SQL Server's features for vertical and horizontal scaling.

Vertical scaling, or scale-up, involves increasing the capacity of a single SQL Server instance by adding more CPU cores, memory, or faster storage. This approach is often the starting point for most SQL Server deployments because it allows for straightforward upgrades without significant changes to the database design or application code. However, vertical scaling has limitations, primarily due to hardware constraints and diminishing returns. At a certain point, adding more resources to a single machine leads to minimal performance gains, especially when the bottlenecks are related to disk I/O latency, contention for locks, or inefficient queries. It becomes necessary to consider how SQL Server handles resource allocation internally, particularly with regards to memory buffers, parallelism, and tempdb management.

Horizontal scaling, or scale-out, represents a more complex but highly effective strategy for achieving scalability. In SQL Server environments, this typically involves distributing the workload across multiple servers or instances. One common scale-out pattern is the use of read replicas, which allows read-only queries to be offloaded from the primary instance to one or more secondary replicas. This is often implemented using Always On Availability Groups, which provide automatic synchronization of data and failover capabilities. Read scale-out can dramatically improve performance for reporting and analytical workloads by reducing contention with transactional queries. However, it requires careful consideration of data freshness, latency between replicas, and the consistency requirements of the application.

Partitioning is another key technique for scalable SQL Server design. Table partitioning enables large tables to be divided into smaller, manageable units called partitions, each stored separately and accessed independently. This improves query performance, particularly for range scans and maintenance operations such as index rebuilds. Partitioning can be based on time, geography, or any logical division of data that aligns with business needs. By distributing data across partitions, SQL Server can optimize query execution by pruning irrelevant partitions during scans. Partitioning also facilitates easier archiving and purging of historical data, which helps maintain high performance over time as the data volume grows.

In addition to partitioning, sharding is a method of scaling SQL Server by distributing data across multiple databases or instances, typically with each shard responsible for a subset of data based on a sharding key. While SQL Server does not natively support sharding out of the box, it can be implemented at the application level or by using frameworks that manage data distribution and routing. Sharding introduces complexity in terms of query routing, cross-shard joins, and transactional consistency, but it provides a powerful way to achieve massive scalability in multi-tenant or globally distributed applications.

Storage architecture plays a critical role in designing scalable SQL Server environments. High-performance storage solutions, such as NVMe-based SSDs and Storage Spaces Direct, can significantly reduce latency and improve throughput. Storage layout strategies, including separating data, log, and tempdb files across different storage volumes, help minimize contention and optimize I/O patterns. In virtualized or cloud-based environments, selecting the right disk types and configuring them with appropriate caching and IOPS limits is essential for maintaining predictable performance. As SQL Server relies heavily on disk performance, especially for transaction logging and tempdb activity, the storage tier must be designed to accommodate peak workloads and ensure consistent response times.

Network infrastructure also affects the scalability of distributed SQL Server architectures. In Always On Availability Groups and log shipping scenarios, the speed and reliability of the network link between replicas determine the synchronization lag and recovery time objectives. High-throughput, low-latency networks are crucial when implementing hybrid architectures that span on-premises and cloud environments. In multi-region deployments, considerations such as data sovereignty, latency, and failover complexity must be addressed to maintain both scalability and compliance.

Monitoring and observability are essential components of a scalable architecture. As the number of SQL Server instances grows, centralized monitoring becomes necessary to maintain visibility and control. Tools such as SQL Server Management Studio, Query Store, Extended Events, and third-party monitoring platforms provide insights into performance trends, query behavior, and resource utilization. Monitoring enables proactive tuning, capacity planning, and detection of issues before they escalate. Scalability is not just about handling more users or data, but about maintaining stable performance under changing conditions, which can only be achieved with real-time insights and historical baselines.

Cloud-based deployments offer a new dimension to SQL Server scalability. Services like Azure SQL Database and Azure SQL Managed Instance provide built-in features such as elastic pools, automatic scaling, and geo-replication, removing much of the operational complexity traditionally associated with scaling. In these environments, compute and storage can scale independently, allowing workloads to adjust dynamically based on demand. Serverless SQL offerings further abstract the underlying infrastructure, automatically allocating resources as queries are executed. This model is ideal for unpredictable or sporadic workloads and simplifies capacity management. When designing for the cloud, considerations shift from provisioning fixed hardware to defining performance tiers and optimizing for cost and efficiency.

Security and compliance must not be overlooked in scalable SQL Server architectures. As the system expands, so does the attack surface. Proper authentication, encryption, and access control become more complex to manage at scale. Role-based access control, transparent data encryption, and audit logging are essential to ensure that security scales with the infrastructure. Additionally, maintaining consistency across multiple instances, whether on-premises or in the cloud, requires configuration management tools and automated deployment pipelines to prevent configuration drift and human error.

Designing scalable SQL Server architectures requires a holistic approach that balances performance, maintainability, cost, and risk. It demands a deep understanding of the SQL Server engine, the ability to forecast growth patterns, and the discipline to implement best practices in a consistent and automated manner. Whether scaling up to more powerful hardware, scaling out across multiple replicas, partitioning data, or migrating to cloud services, the underlying principles remain the same: build with flexibility, plan for change, and optimize continuously. A scalable architecture is not a single solution but a dynamic framework that evolves alongside the applications it supports, ensuring long-term reliability and success.

# Future Trends in SQL Server Administration and Technologies

The future of SQL Server administration and technologies is being shaped by rapid advances in cloud computing, automation, artificial intelligence, and evolving application architectures. As businesses continue to generate and rely on vast amounts of data, SQL Server must adapt to meet changing expectations for performance, scalability, and integration. The traditional role of the database administrator is evolving into that of a data platform engineer, with responsibilities that stretch beyond mere maintenance and monitoring to encompass architecture design, automation scripting, security governance, and cross-platform data mobility. SQL Server, as a product, is also transforming, embracing more flexible deployment models, intelligent features, and cloud-native capabilities that are redefining how organizations build and manage their data infrastructure.

One of the most prominent trends is the increasing adoption of hybrid and multi-cloud environments. Organizations are no longer limited to a single datacenter or cloud provider. SQL Server now plays a central role in distributed architectures that span on-premises servers, virtual machines in the cloud, and fully managed services like Azure SQL Database and Azure SQL Managed Instance. Administrators must become proficient in managing data across these diverse environments, including understanding how to secure, replicate, and synchronize databases in scenarios where latency, bandwidth, and cost vary widely. This flexibility empowers businesses to optimize their workloads for performance, compliance, or budget, but it also requires a new level of strategic planning and architectural awareness.

Automation is rapidly becoming a cornerstone of modern SQL Server administration. Manual, repetitive tasks such as patching, backups, index maintenance, and user provisioning are increasingly being handled by automation frameworks. Tools like PowerShell, Azure CLI, and Infrastructure as Code platforms like Terraform and Bicep are enabling administrators to define, deploy, and manage SQL Server environments with high consistency and repeatability. This trend reduces operational risk, increases efficiency, and frees up database professionals to focus on higher-value activities like performance optimization and data architecture. As automation matures, it is being augmented by artificial intelligence, allowing for predictive analytics that can identify potential issues before they arise and suggest corrective actions based on historical patterns.

Artificial intelligence and machine learning are being embedded into SQL Server itself, most notably through the introduction of intelligent query processing features. Features like adaptive joins, interleaved execution, and automatic plan correction are early examples of how SQL Server is using AI to optimize performance without administrator intervention. The Query Store continues to evolve as a powerful telemetry system, enabling better decision-making about execution plans and regressions. Future versions are expected to deepen this integration, using machine learning models to optimize workloads dynamically, recommend indexes, and even automate query rewriting. These advancements will reduce the time spent on manual tuning and make performance management more accessible to non-expert users.

Another significant shift is the emergence of platform-agnostic SQL Server administration. With the release of SQL Server for Linux and container support through Docker and Kubernetes, SQL Server has become more flexible in terms of deployment environments. Administrators are no longer restricted to Windows Server platforms and can now build containerized, microservice-based applications that include SQL Server as a modular and portable component. This opens the door to DevOps practices like continuous integration and continuous deployment (CI/CD), where database changes are tested and released through automated pipelines. The ability to run SQL Server in containers also improves scalability and disaster recovery, making it easier to spin up replicas and test failover scenarios in isolated environments.

Security and compliance will continue to be major concerns in the future of SQL Server administration. As data privacy regulations become stricter and cyber threats more sophisticated, SQL Server will need to offer more advanced security features. Enhancements in data encryption, secure enclaves, and centralized identity management will become standard. Administrators will be expected to implement zero-trust architectures, enforce least privilege access, and use tools like Azure Defender for SQL and Microsoft Purview to monitor and audit data usage. Automated threat detection and response systems will become integral to SQL Server environments, enabling real-time identification of anomalous activity and rapid mitigation of potential breaches.

Edge computing is emerging as a frontier where SQL Server is beginning to play a role. In scenarios where data must be processed close to the source for reasons of latency or connectivity, lightweight versions of SQL Server can be deployed on edge devices. These instances can perform local analytics, data filtering, and synchronization with central databases. This distributed model supports applications in fields such as manufacturing, logistics, and healthcare, where real-time data access and decision-making are critical. As IoT adoption grows, the need for robust yet compact SQL Server deployments at the edge will drive new innovations in storage, replication, and synchronization technologies.

Cloud-native analytics and big data integration are also influencing the evolution of SQL Server. Features like PolyBase and Azure Synapse Link are enabling SQL Server to interact seamlessly with external data sources, including Hadoop clusters, blob storage, and real-time event streams. This integration allows SQL Server to act as both a transactional system and an analytical engine, reducing the traditional gap between operational and analytical data. In the future, SQL Server is expected to include even deeper hooks into data lakes, stream processing engines, and machine learning services, making it a central component of unified data platforms. Administrators will need to understand data pipelines, ETL/ELT processes, and data visualization tools to fully leverage these capabilities.

Licensing and pricing models are also expected to evolve in response to the shift towards consumption-based computing. Instead of purchasing perpetual licenses or committing to fixed capacities, organizations may increasingly opt for pay-as-you-go models that align costs with actual usage. SQL Server in Azure already supports this model, and future offerings may provide even more granular billing options, such as charging based on query volume, transaction throughput, or compute time. This change will require administrators to develop financial acumen, as cost optimization becomes a key performance metric alongside uptime and response time.

The future of SQL Server administration is one of continuous transformation. Administrators must evolve their skills to stay relevant, embracing new tools, programming paradigms, and architectural patterns. Collaboration with developers, security teams, and cloud architects will become more important than ever. SQL Server is no longer just a storage engine for relational data; it is becoming a foundational platform for intelligent, resilient, and scalable data-driven applications. By keeping pace with these changes, administrators can not only ensure the stability and performance of SQL Server systems but also drive innovation and strategic value across the entire organization.

www.ingramcontent.com/pod-product-compliance
Lightning Source LLC
LaVergne TN
LVHW022314060326
832902LV00020B/3456